MORE PRAISE FOR
IN SEARCH OF THE COLOR PURPLE

"Salamishah does what only great writers of literary criticism accomplish—she tells a story about a masterpiece without forgetting the extraordinary woman who crafted it and the legions of women made whole because of her work. A bold and vital tale that rightly treats Alice Walker's American classic as if it were a living, breathing being demanding our utmost attention and enduring affection."

—JANET MOCK, AUTHOR OF
REDEFINING REALNESS AND *SURPASSING CERTAINTY*

"This book is a stunning act of devotion, a literary and personal excavation of one of the great novels of American literature, *The Color Purple* . . . . Salamishah has allowed this extraordinary work of fiction to guide and heal her life, and her book does the same for us."

—EVE ENSLER, AUTHOR OF
THE VAGINA MONOLOGUES AND *THE APOLOGY*

IN SEARCH OF
THE COLOR PURPLE

ALSO BY SALAMISHAH TILLET:

Sites of Slavery:
Citizenship and Racial Democracy in the Post–Civil Rights Imagination

SALAMISHAH
TILLET

IN SEARCH OF
THE COLOR PURPLE

THE STORY
OF AN
AMERICAN
MASTERPIECE

ABRAMS PRESS, NEW YORK

Library of Congress Control Number: 2018958796

ISBN: 978-1-4197-3530-1
eISBN: 978-1-68335-685-1

Printed and bound in the United States
10 9 8 7 6 5 4 3 2 1

Abrams books are available at special discounts when purchased in quantity for premiums and promotions as well as fundraising or educational use. Special editions can also be created to specification. For details, contact specialsales@abramsbooks.com or the address below.

Abrams Press® is a registered trademark of Harry N. Abrams, Inc.

ABRAMS The Art of Books
195 Broadway, New York, NY 10007
abramsbooks.com

To my sister Scheherazade, without whom I would not have
been able to pick up the pieces and make myself whole again

&

To my entire A Long Walk Home family,
whose work to free us of sexual violence makes my faith possible

Healing begins where the wound was made.

—ALICE WALKER

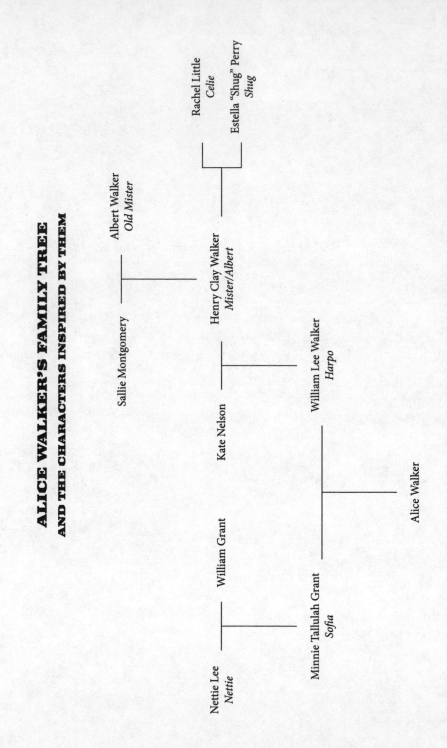

ALICE WALKER'S FAMILY TREE
AND THE CHARACTERS INSPIRED BY THEM

Sallie Montgomery

Albert Walker
Old Mister

Henry Clay Walker
Mister/Albert

Kate Nelson

Rachel Little
Celie

Estella "Shug" Perry
Shug

William Lee Walker
Harpo

William Grant

Nettie Lee
Nettie

Minnie Tallulah Grant
Sofia

Alice Walker

CONTENTS

FOREWORD
BY GLORIA STEINEM

YOU ARE ABOUT TO READ the life story of *The Color Purple*, from the day Celie and Shug came alive in Alice Walker's imagination and asked for a quiet country place to be born, to a book, a movie, a musical, another play, and, finally, a worldwide life right up there with all the classics.

That is the mega-history of *The Color Purple*. But what is even more rare is how it weaves into the fabric of our own lives.

I was on a long plane trip when I first read *The Color Purple*. Because I was lucky to have Alice as a friend and a colleague, her people entered my life even before they inhabited a book. I was doubly lucky, because the long time span and intimacy of a plane trip allowed me to stay in their world until it came to a natural end.

In that magical time cocoon, Celie transformed herself from the downest and outest of women to a free spirit who helped others to be free. Shug became an agent of that freedom, as well as a miracle of strength, sensuality, and a new freedom within herself.

Even Mister, who begins as Celie's cruel master, gradually becomes more understandable when we learn about his suffering at the hands of a cruel father. By the end, Mister isn't perfect, but he has become a person who enables others to be free.

Such transformation is pure Alice. She never gives up on anyone, in her imagination or in real life, and so she allows each of us to become better human beings. Imagination always paves the way to reality.

So, by the time I emerged from the cocoon of that plane ride and *The Color Purple*, I knew I would do pretty much anything to help more people enter the world Alice had created, partly from her own family myths and stories, and partly from dreams.

In the book you are about to read, Salamishah Tillet picks up the story of *The Color Purple* as it is published and explains the slowness of the publisher in realizing that this was a book for the whole country and the world. It was a resistance to the miraculous by people expecting the ordinary. Publishing also tends to apply adjectives to authors, and a black woman writer must be limited and special, not limitless and universal.

It's interesting that publishers, scholars, and critics so often assume that white males, like the Russian Tolstoy or the French Proust, are great writers Americans will understand and love. Yet, they may resist the idea that a black woman writer, who shares their country and language, will have a universal appeal here and around the world.

Fortunately, readers refused to be predicted by those publishers and critics.

But, to come back to my own personal history with *The Color Purple*: there were two accidental moments when I realized that this book about poor people in the rural American South would really be universal for people everywhere. Both were also meetings related to traveling, which, as you can see, I do a lot of.

First, I was in Tokyo and happened to meet Yumiko Yanagisawa, who had translated *The Color Purple* into Japanese. She had fallen in love with the simplicity of Alice's writing, and somehow managed to convey this in her own more formal and ancient language. I couldn't imagine how this was possible, since Alice wrote as her people spoke, without even the quotation marks and apostrophes that, in this country, let the reader and the writer share the superior knowledge that this was a dialect, not standard English. Yumiko told me with tears in her eyes that she believed it was the first time such simplicity was the unapologetic entirety of a great novel.

Second, I met accidentally in an airport a woman who was translating Alice's novel into Chinese. Amazingly, she told me a parallel story. She had chosen some part of rural China for the language of its countrypeople, whose speech also had not been used in a great novel or serious literature before.

Ever since then, I've wondered if that translation included words from the famous Nüshu writing invented by women in Hunan Province. Forbidden to go to school, they used this secret woman-only written language to send letters to each other. Many letters have survived, even though their correspondence was so precious that these women were often buried with letters from their women friends.

If so, I bet Celie and Shug would have loved the idea of this, the only woman-invented written language in the world, carrying their story. It seems just like the letters Celie wrote to God when she had no other friend, and then to her sister once she discovered her existence.

I tell you these stories from distant countries because they made me realize something important. If you create one true thing, it stays true wherever it goes.

Of course, truth-telling also gets punished. Revealing the

violence of some black men toward black women also brought Alice great pain, as you will read in these pages. Interestingly, she was less punished for telling the truth in a book than she was when that book was made into a movie. It's as if the fierce black male critics who condemned her were less angered by disclosing a truth than by how many people had heard it.

I was shocked by the viciousness of criticism Alice had suffered at the time. Reading about it in this book, I am alarmed all over again by the painful punishment Alice endured for her truth-telling. From Sophocles to Shakespeare, we have been warned that the bearer of bad news will be punished, yet I wasn't at all prepared to see Alice suffer. Some of her suffering was salt in wounds long inflicted on black men by racism, while some of it stems from the fact that we not only live in a patriarchy, but that patriarchy also lives in us.

I suspect that oppression may result in more fear of criticism, even when it comes from our own.

Altogether, *The Color Purple* had and continues to have a profound impact on my life, as I suspect it does on all the lives it enters.

So when Salamishah Tillet told me she wanted to tell a story, as if the book were a person, I knew this was crucial to do. I also knew she was the right person to do it.

As with Alice, I first came to know Salamishah through her writing. In her case, she wrote essays that illuminated current events, as if they were prisms she held up to the light, and also stories of her own life that helped other women as only truth can. As with Alice, her writing made me want to meet her. We became friends and learned about each other's lives.

Though there is a difference in age between Salamishah and Alice, these two women share so much as writers, activists, feminists, survivors, mothers, and leaders. As someone even older than Alice, I also told Salamishah how I feel about meeting great younger women: *I just had to wait for some of my friends to be born.*

I was honored to be a bridge between Salamishah and Alice, and now to this life story of *The Color Purple.*

I bet you will tell it to many more.

INTRODUCTION:
LOOKING FOR ALICE

SHE DOESN'T HAVE A MULE, but Alice Walker does have her forty acres. Sitting atop the lush vineyards of Mendocino County's Anderson Valley, her house had a view of an endless sweep of low mountains, the highest of which the locals here call Signal Ridge. Walker, however, in honor of the indigenous communities of the area, calls it Mount Pomo. "When I wake up in the morning, I can't see anything at all," Alice says. "The fog stretches across the entire valley and that's all you can see." By lunchtime, when my sister, Scheherazade, and I arrived at her house, the fog had receded and only rolling, lush green tops stretched away from us. Now at its peak, the sun hovered right above us. It was so rejuvenating that I forgot how exhausted I was from our cross-country flight to San Francisco and our more than three-hour journey by car northwest to Alice's house near Philo, a town of less than four hundred people.

I was there because of *The Color Purple*, the novel for which Walker, in 1983, won the National Book Award and became the first black woman to win the Pulitzer Prize in fiction. Since then, the book has sold more than five million copies and has been translated into more than two dozen languages. The director Steven Spielberg adapted it to the big screen for a 1985 release, which in turn generated approximately $142 million in box office sales and earned eleven Oscar nominations, including Best Picture. Twenty years later, Oprah Winfrey, who made her screen debut in the movie as Sofia, produced it on Broadway. The musical was such a sales bonanza that audiences bought more than $5 million worth of show souvenirs in 2006 alone, five times what a typical show might make. Its success led to a national tour, a revival of the show in London, a Tony Award–winning Broadway revival in 2015, starring Jennifer Hudson and Cynthia Erivo, an ongoing national tour today, and, most recently, Spielberg and Winfrey have teamed up with producer Scott Sanders to make a movie of the musical which slated for release in 2022.

Despite her story's vast appeal to readers, movie watchers, and playgoers, Alice could only write *The Color Purple* in one place. The characters Celie, Shug, and Sofia started to appear to her in the late 1970s while she lived in Brooklyn—on subways, on dark streets, and especially in the shadow of skyscrapers—but they refused to stay with her for long. "What is this tall shit anyway?" they'd ask her. So she moved. First to San Francisco, and when her protagonists continued to complain about the earthquakes, she went even farther north. One day, after passing an African American boy cheerfully walking on the side of the road in Boonville, California, she and Robert Allen, the editor of the journal the *Black Scholar* and her partner of twelve years, looked at the local listings and eventually rented a house. Walker later told her biographer, "I figured that any place where a black child looked that happy and carefree was probably a good place to live."

But Alice Walker was the only other black person besides me and my sister that I saw during our three-day pilgrimage there. That fact felt off-putting. Boonville had existed in my mind for so long as the literary birthplace of *The Color Purple* that I half expected it to be a doppelgänger for Eatonton, Georgia, Alice's birthplace and the setting of her most famous novel. Instead, Boonville was mainly white, and a bit Latinx, and closer to the sparse landscape of Robert Mailer Anderson's 2001 debut novel, *Boonville*, in which he describes a main strip checkered with a gas station, bar, market, hotel, diner, coffee shop, another bar, and an open highway. And beyond that, Mailer writes, is "a slab of concrete wedged between hills and trees, winding away from what he thought must have been a mirage."

WALKER FILLED IN THOSE FISSURES with a kaleidoscope of southern black life. For her, Boonville *did* feel like Eatonton, "only it was more beautiful, and the swimming hole was not segregated." In her 1983 essay "Writing *The Color Purple*," Walker recalled, "Seeing the sheep, the cattle, and the goats, smelling the apples and the hay, one of my characters, Celie, began, haltingly, to speak." Soon after, the others arrived. And this time, they stayed. As Alice sat in her one-room cottage facing a meadow and an apple orchard and sought guidance from the river and among the redwoods in that year of 1980, her characters not only came to life but also began to fall in love with each other and even with Walker herself.

The unforeseen success of her writing enabled Walker to buy her first twenty acres near Philo, a few miles up from Boonville. As we curved along 128, I flashed back to a photograph of Walker's studio that was on the front cover of her essay collection *Anything We Love Can Be Saved*, a book that I bought immediately upon graduating from college in 1996. In the image, Walker is looking right into the lens assuredly. She's in her early fifties in the photo, and her signature dark brown locks fall shortly over her shoulders. Wearing a knitted cap, patterned black sweater, washed-out jeans, and rain boots, Walker stands in front of wood shingles and bronze pots with skin that glistens. This was a place—and a woman—that had loomed large in my mind for many years.

The first time I read *The Color Purple*, I was fifteen years old and spending the summer in Boston with my dad, preparing to apply for early decision to the University of Pennsylvania. I had just been let go from my part-time canvassing gig at an environmental law center because my boss realized that I was too young to be knocking on people's doors well past dusk. Since it was too late for me to pick up another summer job, I ended up answering phones, sorting mail, and volunteering at the local NAACP office.

During my breaks I'd pick up the latest of the weekly books that my cousin's tall, light-brown-skinned girlfriend, Nicole, gave me to read. She was only two years older than I was but already an English major at Penn herself, and sensing that I was on the verge of an identity crisis, she felt obligated to help me build up my armor of African American literature. In turn, three books in particular determined my fate: Alex Haley's *The Autobiography of Malcolm X*, Toni Morrison's *The Bluest Eye*, and Alice Walker's *The Color Purple*. By the time I returned home to New Jersey and to my suburban private high school that fall, I felt armed with a new vocabulary of racial pride and black feminism.

Walker's protagonist, Celie Harris, a dark-brown-skinned African American girl born in segregation, made the book all the more fascinating to me. "Dear God," Celie opens the novel, "I am fourteen years old. I am I have always been a good girl. Maybe you can give me a sign letting me know what is happening to me."

4

What Celie was unable to name was the fact that the man she called Pa repeatedly raped her as her enfeebled mother wasted away in the next room. "You better not tell nobody but God," he warns. "It'd kill your mammy." By creating a protagonist who was a victim of racism and repeated rapes—and also a figure who eventually was able to break her silence and tell her story on her own terms—Walker turned Celie into one of the most original characters in all of literature.

I've gone back to *The Color Purple* many times since that summer of 1991: after I was raped by an African American fraternity boy whom I was dating during my first year of college, and again after I was sexually assaulted by a near stranger on my college study abroad program in Kenya. Years later, after struggling with an eating disorder, contemplating suicide, and going to intensive therapy, I poured out all my anger and heartache in my poem "Do You Know What Rape Feels Like." As I retold my trauma, I leaned directly on Walker's words. Midway through my poem, I began, in great detail, to break down the intimate horror of my rape.

> *Do you know what it feels like to have our howls silenced by*
> * a fist?*
> *When you are rushed into, pressed down on and opened by*
> * a knife.*
> *A blade so thick, so strong, so brilliant*
> *That your insides no longer exist.*
> *Your scraped against insides bleed out into a yell*
> *That only you*
> *And others like you can hear?*

Screaming until it stops
No, until you think it stops.
And then from nowhere, from no-one, it keeps on.
He continues to destroy your petals, with his -----.
You don't even want to say it.

I broke my silence because of *The Color Purple*. At every stage of my healing, I've found something new in the novel, unseen themes or turns of phrase, that I ignored in my previous visits. When my sister asked if she could document my healing with her camera, I handed my poem over to her. A few months later, when she adapted her photographs and my story into the stage performance *Story of a Rape Survivor*, our actress, Rachel Walker, gave life to my words and let Celie's words be her creative guide. If Celie gave voice to my rape in my teens and early twenties, it was Shug, in her bawdiness and bodily confidence, whom I needed in my thirties as I entered a belated phase of sexual experimentation and exploration. And among the pantheon of black women characters whom I introduced to my students when I first started teaching at the University of Pennsylvania, Shug meant the most to me. Her sexual fluidity and unabashed desires gave me permission to experiment unapologetically with men and women and long for more.

Now, I live differently with *The Color Purple*. A lot more healed, yet still tender, I revel in Sofia's anger. Her rage at being doubly oppressed as black *and* a woman fuels me as I raise and protect my black children, a five-year-old boy and an eight-year-old girl, in our age of unbridled racism. In the book, but especially on-screen and onstage, Sofia captures my attention and dares me to be more like her. This is why every time I pick up the novel, even the one I teach from, covered by pastel stickies and with its dog-eared pages, I feel as if it is for the very first time, finding and falling in love with a new moment that I somehow missed before.

I tried not to carry the enormousness of the novel's meaning for me when I finally met Alice Walker. I wasn't sure if I should remain professionally detached and not disclose my own experiences with sexual assault. Or if I should tell her that I'd read every poem, essay, short story, and novel that she'd published since 1970 and that she, more than any artist I'd discovered before or after her, gave me permission as a black woman to be a full-fledged feminist. I was so afraid that my euphoria would spill out or that I'd fumble, that when my sister and I approached her Haiku-inspired house standing at the top of the hill, with only a bunch of periwinkles standing between us and her, I did not hug Alice or thank her for writing the book that made my healing possible. Instead, I put on my writer's cap, introduced my sister as a photographer, and began to take notes.

Gone were Alice's long locks. Now, a short silver mane crowned her head and she walked with an unbelievable lightness. And when she took us out onto the back porch of "Temple Jook," the name that she used for her house in our email correspondence, we three black women stood silently together. Alice, on the verge of her seventy-fifth birthday; Scheherazade, a newly minted forty-year-old; and I, a month into my forty-fourth year, looked out to see only a crescendo of mountains standing between us and the horizon.

After a minute, a deep inhale, and with a wry smile on her face, Walker asked, "Why do we need heaven when we have this?" And when I turned my head to catch her question, I realized that Alice Walker was the freest black woman I'd ever met.

≈≈≈

UNLIKE ME, Alice was not trying to impress. Before sitting on the couch to begin my interview, I slipped off my burgundy boots, which, known only to Scheherazade, I had just put on in her driveway. In contrast to me in my light-yellow silk Cynthia Rowley minidress, Alice looked supremely casual in leather sandals, black knit pants, and a cotton striped T-shirt. She struck me as the type of person who long ago discovered that her body was hers alone.

I'd met a black woman like her once before. On her long walk home after she killed her lover. With a long braid swinging down her faded shirt and muddy overalls, Janie Crawford, the heroine of Zora Neale Hurston's 1937 novel, *Their Eyes Were Watching God*. Of her homecoming, Hurston wrote that Janie was "full of that oldest human longing—self-revelation." Despite leaving one husband, being widowed by an even wealthier one, and having to shoot her rabid and homicidal boyfriend to death during a hurricane in the Everglades, when Hurston's heroine returned back home to Eatonville, Florida, she did so with such quiet confidence that her fellow black townspeople could only envy, not pity, Janie. Despite arriving on the literary scene to much delight and debate during the Harlem Renaissance, when Hurston died in 1960, both she and her work had fallen into obscurity.

Walker, in part, resurrected Hurston's legacy. In 1975, in *Ms.* magazine, she published an essay called "Looking for Zora," in which she described pretending to be Zora's niece and walking around Hurston's all-black hometown of Eatonville in search of some sign of Hurston's legacy there. Tragically, because Hurston spent her final years working as a domestic and later died impoverished and in a welfare home, she was known only to the octogenarian Mathilda Moseley, her former classmate and the teller of the "woman-is-smarter-than-man" tales in Hurston's *Mules and Men*. Moseley guided Walker to Hurston's grave site ninety minutes away at the Garden of Heavenly Rest in Fort Pierce, Florida. There, among the snakes and thigh-high weeds, Alice found an unmarked grave. "There are times—and finding Zora Hurston's grave was one of them," Alice wrote, "when normal responses of grief, horror and so on do not make sense because they bear no real relation to the depth of emotion one feels." Before leaving, Alice bought a headstone that read, "Zora Neale Hurston: A genius of the South. Novelist. Folklorist. Anthropologist."

I knew none of this when I read Hurston's novel, the only one by an African American author that I'd read in my high school in the early 1990s. By then, scholars had already tethered *Their Eyes* and *The Color Purple* to each other. In 1988, for example, Henry Louis Gates Jr. theorized in his book of literary criticism *The Signifying Monkey* that Walker was determined for Celie to speak in her own voice in order to pay homage to Hurston and counter the claim that *Their Eyes* was flawed because most of the novel was written in the third person. Noting Walker's increasing emphasis on first-person narration, Gates wrote, "For Celie it is the written voice which is her vehicle for self-expression and self-revelation."

Even Harold Bloom, best known for his "anxiety of influence" theory, which espoused that literary texts were always anxious creative responses to those that preceded them, suspended the combative aspect of his thesis for Walker. Writing in 1995, Bloom asserted, "Walker, whether in *The Color Purple* or *Meridian,* is very much Zora Neale Hurston's novelistic daughter." By the time I began teaching my own African American literature courses, reading them as family was such standard practice that I always taught the two books together, sitting them next to each other like sisters. In all my years of teaching these authors, I never once questioned their lineage.

"I don't think I'm in the tradition of Zora, actually," Alice Walker says to me.

I reply in disbelief, "Huh, that's interesting."

"It's hard to explain, really, because I adore her, and I'm happy to be in it," she flatly says after a few seconds. "And people associate me with her; I did so much work in claiming her. But I think in many ways, we're very different."

"Did I misread that connection?"

"I think it's so easy to feel this way because there's so many similarities, but I saw claiming her and adoring her and pressing her forward as just my duty. In the same way that—not exactly in the same way, but kind of in a way—I feel about the characters in *The Color Purple*. That they didn't have a voice."

And that's when I notice my mistake. The woman sitting across from me bears little resemblance to Zora in late life. In fact, Walker seems to be acutely aware of their personal and ideological differences and to be consciously defying Hurston's fate. She has claimed her own land, shaped her resting place, and kept almost every letter, card, manuscript, and journal that she has received or written. Given her relentless commitment to self-archiving, I wonder out loud if she always knew someone like me might go on a quest to find her.

"What I knew," she responds, "was that I had a responsibility to those after me and if I could be helpful by leaving a map, that's what I'd do."

It took her a few years, but Walker eventually bought the other twenty acres of Philo land. After our first set of interviews, a noticeably worn-out Walker offered Scheherazade and me an opportunity to walk around the grounds of her estate. Because a recent guest of hers broke their ankle on the path and had to be airlifted by helicopter to a nearby hospital, she insisted that we each choose one of her walking sticks. Leaving my boots behind, I opted for the black suede sneakers in which I had driven and began to follow my sister on the trail.

It was only after Scheherazade and I took a tour of the property, walking past the garden with the chickens and collard greens, swaying on the wooden swings outside, curling up on the bed inside of her one-room tree house, and starting back up the hill, past the pond and the swimming pool, that I realized how much I originally missed in our stroll down. In the mainhouse, Alice has another guest room with a larger than life black-and-white print of Frida Kahlo, the artist's head covered and facing downward, hanging on the wall. The only other image in the room that compares in size and significance is a sepia-toned portrait of Walker herself. It is the image that graces the back of the most recent edition of *The Color Purple*. Beneath that photograph sits an antique writer's desk with a turquoise marbled lamp, a canister of pens and pencils, and a row of either the first or her favorite editions of her novels. On the far left, three different editions of *The Color Purple* humbly sit next to the other, their repetition a mark of the novel's reach.

Almost immediately upon the novel's publication in 1982, dissenters panned its use of a black dialect and its celebration of lesbianism. The harshest criticism came from other writers, mainly black men who accused Walker of reproducing racist stereotypes of them as hyperviolent rapists. While the writer Ishmael Reed later refuted calling *The Color Purple* "a Nazi conspiracy," he did blast the book and the film in interview after interview. He even satirized Walker in *Reckless Eyeballing*, his 1986 novel that turned Walker into the fictional character Tremonisha Smarts, who gains fame for writing *Wrongheaded Man*, a play about a black man who goes around bashing and raping women that is so successful that the white feminist theater producer Barbara Sedgwick wants to adapt it into a movie. As the plot unfolds, Reed's real aim is clear. He creates an unknown assailant he calls "the Flower Phantom" who ties up Tremonisha and shaves her head bald, a punishment he modeled after the French Resistance, which used to shave the heads of women who collaborated with the Nazis.

That criticism only grew more vociferous with the release of Spielberg's film adaptation. The journalist Tony Brown dedicated an entire episode of his weekly television program in April 1986 to the film (after claiming never to have seen it) and expressed concern that Spielberg's picture would "become the only statement on black men" from the majority white Hollywood. Later Brown told *Newsweek* it was "the most anti-black family film of the modern film era." In an interview with the *New York Times* to promote *She's Gotta Have It*, Spike Lee said, "The difference between this film and 'The Color Purple' is that even though there are some dog black men in this film, you can tell there is a difference. This film was not done with hate, and none of the men here are one-note animals, like Mister."

Protesting what they saw as the savage and brutal depictions of black men in the film, an activist group named the Coalition Against Black Exploitation picketed the December 1985 premiere of *The Color Purple* in Los Angeles. The message that these and other columnists and law professors and even some representatives of the NAACP sent was clear: Walker had betrayed her race by depicting her black male characters as abusers and by giving permission to Spielberg, a young, white, Jewish director, to put it on the big screen. Despite its being nominated for eleven Academy Awards, the pushback was so massive that the film did not win one Oscar.

"No writer in the twentieth century was attacked in the sustained and virulent way that Alice was around this novel. No writer. None," said the late Rudolph Byrd, a professor of American and African American studies at Emory College and the founding co-chair of the Alice Walker Literary Society. The critique was that Alice Walker and her novel were committed only to an unfair representation of black men. Feminists at that time were perceived—and are still perceived—as hostile to the black liberation struggle. Walker's good friend and Spelman College feminist professor Beverly Guy-Sheftall said it even more plainly to me: "Alice was the most hated black woman in America. Ever."

To work through it, Walker retreated to Northern California and continued to write, even publishing a novel that, through Celie and Shug's granddaughter, Fanny, continues the arc of *The Color Purple*. Reflecting in her journal in December 1986, Walker said, "My new novel is coming along. Good people, interesting sinners." She went on, "I think I will call the novel something that came to me in a dream: *The Temple of My Familiar*, and Celie and Shug will maybe drift through, and we can see what becomes of them." At the same time, she also turned inward for protection and self-preservation, an experience that she says strengthened her spiritually. When Scheherazade and I returned to our hotel after our first day with Walker, we confessed how much we didn't want to leave her. By merely sitting with Alice, I felt like she was transferring energy to me, grounding me in her presence and my skin.

"My novel *The Color Purple* was actually my Buddha novel without Buddhism," Walker asserted in a 2002 talk at the Spirit Rock Meditation Center. "In the face of unbearable suffering following the assassinations and betrayals of the civil rights movement, I too sat down upon the Earth and asked its permission to posit a different way from that in which I was raised." Unlike Wards Chapel, the African Methodist Episcopal church in which Walker grew up, her novel explored a viable alternative to Christian dogma: Nature. In the preface to the twenty-fifth anniversary edition, Walker wrote, "It is no mystery how and at what point in time African Americans, like the characters in this novel, began believing in a God designed to guide and further the desires of another people, a God who thought of blackness as a curse." Celie's journey is as much about her communion with nature as it is a coming-of-age story. Or, as Walker says of her heroine, "Everything that happens during her life, spanning decades, is in relation to her growth in understanding this force." And yet, despite the centrality of spirituality in *The Color Purple*, Walker, twenty-five years later, was left to query why the novel is "so infrequently discussed as a book about God."

By the end of the book, however, Celie narrates, "Dear God, dear stars, dear trees, dear sky, dear peoples. Dear Everything. Dear God," and comes full circle with her journey to self and community. Like Celie's own rebirth, *The Color Purple* continues to reemerge, with each iteration serving as a new and often even sharper reflection of the time in which it appears, enabling the novel to have a literary timelessness *and* a political timeliness that few American

bildungsromans have achieved. The rise and fall of the novel's original bold politics parallels black women's political journeys to the
center of American life, with each subsequent version, for better or
for worse, inspiring and being inspired by the zeitgeist.

In Search of The Color Purple is my retelling of that journey. This is a book not only about how Alice Walker birthed her
masterpiece but also about how her singular story shaped—and
continues to shape—generations of readers who've found solace
and sisterhood by embracing Celie. The path that Walker gives
us in *The Color Purple*, from Celie's original trauma to her sexual awakening with Shug, from eventual forgiveness of Albert to
final reconnection with her sister, her children, and to the God
in everything and everyone, is not merely character growth but
a model for our healing and transformation from oppressed sub-
jects to empowered citizens.

This is why I believe the novel's main black women characters—Celie, Shug, and Sofia—have endured and emerged as
guides that have imprinted themselves on me to help me heal.
Because Celie is Walker's main protagonist, her heroine, she is
the character with whom I open this book as I trace how Walker
turned to her own life and family history as inspiration for the
novel's assortment of characters, particularly her stepgrandmother, Rachel Walker, for Celie and her grandfather Henry Clay
Walker for Albert. In Part I, "Celie," I meditate on the personal
details and artistic development in Walker's young life that prepared her to write *The Color Purple*; spend time with Walker's
various drafts of the novel and her correspondence with her
editors; and consider the literary innovation and heritage that
Walker drew on to birth Celie in the American literary canon in
1982.

If Celie is the character in whom I saw myself as a teenager, Shug is who I wanted to be as a young woman. She is African American literature's most famous bisexual black female character and exudes such fullness and sexual control that she seemed to me everything I was not. In the days before I was raped, Shug represented sexual fluidity and endless possibility. In the years after, I found myself, like Celie, to be in a state of longing, hoping that by simply reading the novel over and over again, I'd pick up Shug's self-confidence and bodily agency.

Clearly, not everyone felt the same way.

In Part II, "Shug," I discuss the controversy that began brewing with the novel's publication and Walker's garnering of the most prestigious literary awards in America—the Pulitzer Prize and the National Book Award—and came to a head with the 1985 release of the movie *The Color Purple*. That film, produced by Quincy Jones and directed by Steven Spielberg, is the heart of the second part of this book, for more than any other of Walker's characters it is Shug, with her unbridled social and sexual freedom, who prompted outrage, threats of boycott, and censorship by critics who saw Celie and Shug's sexual relationship as harmful to depictions of black men on-screen and in the larger society.

I recall the intensity and adverse impact of this controversy on Walker's life and the film's Academy Award chances, as well as feature original interviews with the black men most intimately involved in the making of the film—Jones and Danny Glover—and explore how they responded to such claims then and now. Finally, I look at Shug's and Celie's legacies: first, as recurring characters in Walker's own 1989 novel, *The Temple of My Familiar*, and now as they continue to inspire for black women artists, such as Mickalene Thomas, who found the language to name her own black queer desire for the very first time when she saw two black women loving each other on the silver screen.

Part III is devoted to Sofia, who became so popular over the years that by the time *The Color Purple* appeared on Broadway in 2005, it was she, not Celie's sister, Nettie, who completed this triangle of women. Featuring original interviews with Oprah Winfrey, the actress and icon who made her film debut playing Sofia, as well as the musical producer Scott Sanders and the director John Doyle, these concluding chapters look at how Sofia remains one of the most iconic voices of black resistance and refusal in print *and* on-screen because she embodies the political emotion of our moment—black women's righteous anger—so much so that her movie monologue was the catalyst for Kendrick Lamar's song "Alright," the unofficial anthem of Black Lives Matter. Here, I also consider how, through Albert's path to redemption, Walker gave us a model of male accountability and atonement that we still have yet to achieve in the #MeToo era.

"We will never have to be other than who we are in order to be successful," Celie reminds us. "We realize that we are as ourselves unlimited and our experiences valid. It is for the rest of the world to recognize this, if they choose."

In my research and road trips, my interviews and pilgrimages, I come across people—black and white, men and women, young and old, queer and straight—who all have found themselves in Celie's own journey to self. They, like me, still hold on to the moment of revelation like a talisman and see *The Color Purple* as the ultimate book to which we should all turn in our weary and dystopic times.

As the #MeToo movement has taken hold, millions of survivors of sexual violence have come forward with their own stories of sexual assault. Despite the fact that this usage of the term "me too" was coined by a black woman, Tarana Burke, to help African American girls like the thirteen-year-old in Alabama who told her in 1997 about being sexually abused by her mother's boyfriend, black girls and women victims continue to find themselves at risk for being ignored or rendered invisible, or, as was Walker's fate after the release of the movie, indicted by other black people for perpetuating racist stereotypes about black male sexuality, or for colluding with an unfair criminal justice system if they claim to have been assaulted by an African American man. As a result, the vulnerability of black girls and women, and the ongoing backlash that they publicly receive—as in the cases of those allegedly assaulted by Bill Cosby, Russell Simmons, or R. Kelly—or privately experience—as in the cases of hundreds of black girls and young women whom my sister and I have worked with in our black feminist organization, A Long Walk Home— means that we, as a society, remain disinterested in the fates of millions in order to protect a chosen few. No other writer has been able to imagine the whole arc—the breaking of the silence; the coming to terms with how sexual trauma has impacted individual survivors, their children, and their communities; and the means by which assailants can seek real accountability for their actions, make amends, and ultimately be forgiven—than Alice Walker. Her perspective, though unique, was also shaped by her particular vantage point as a black woman. "Naturally, I write about the things I know best, from the angle I know best," Alice said in an interview while on the set of *The Color Purple* movie in 1985. "Black women have a different angle from which to write, they see things from a different point of view. Black women have to look out and through all those people who have traditionally been on top of them: the black man, the white woman, the white man." She concluded, "This creates a different way of looking at reality."

Through her purple-hued looking glass, Walker imagined a world and created a novel that remains potent, ever prophetic, and a reminder of how far we, as a nation, still really have to go, while being an extraordinary vision of who we want to be.

"What else is there to say about *The Color Purple*?" Walker exhaustedly asks me at the end of our first interview.

Without skipping a beat, I reply:

"Everything."

PART I

_____

CELIE

1. THE LOVELINESS
OF HER SPIRIT

THAT NEXT MORNING, Scheherazade and I walked around the grounds of Alice Walker's home with a newfound familiarity. After we'd eaten two meals with her and even napped in her Frida Kahlo–inspired "Casa Azul" guesthouse the day before, our bond with Alice felt so real and so intense that my sister and I did not want to leave, worried that our recently discovered centeredness would dissolve as we drove away. So, once again, I started plotting, secretly planning another encounter with her, hoping that Alice Walker liked us as much as we adored her.

When she opened the door this time, Alice gave us permission to saunter. Scheherazade was now free to photograph Walker's home, her library, her writing room, and even an altar outside her kitchen that stood in the place of a welcome table. Back in New Jersey, next to my bed, I too have an altar. Mine hosts white candles, a shot glass of rum, a grapefruit, signed first edition copies of *The Color Purple* and Toni Morrison's *Beloved*, an original LP with Nina Simone's "Mississippi Goddam," and photographs of my grandfather Antonio as well as my brother, Shaka, and my grandmothers, Hilda and Luretha Lee, all of whom died in 2013. In contrast, Walker's altar had a group of photographs: a small picture of Alice smiling with her friends and the feminist icons

Gloria Steinem and Wilma Mankiller; a 1930s black-and-white portrait of her parents, Minne Lou Grant and Willie Lee Walker, taken during a rare date night out in Eatonton; and a faded image of an elderly black woman sporting a thick ankle-length skirt, embroidered jacket, and a wooden cane. This was Mary Poole, Walker's great-great-great-great grandmother, who walked to Putnam County after surviving being sold on the auction block and years of enslavement in Virginia. In the 1880s, Mary traveled all those miles in a slave coffle with one baby on each hip.

Through this tapestry of photographs, Walker conveyed those histories—feminist and familial—that were sacred to her. In response to my question about Rachel "Ma Ma" Walker, her step-grandmother and the woman upon whom she based the character Celie, she admits that she could not find the lone photograph that she has of her. "She just looks like a model," Walker says. "Which is to say that she's slender where everybody else was big and she's handsome, so handsome." Walker's insistence on Rachel's beauty doesn't square with how others, including the actresses who've played Celie, experience the role. In her most recent collection of poetry, *Taking the Arrow Out of the Heart*, Walker addressed this head-on in the poem called "Is Celie Actually Ugly?," which she dedicated to Cynthia Erivo, the British actress who won a Tony in 2016 for her portrayal of Celie in the Broadway revival of the musical. Critiquing those of us cruel enough to pose that question in the first place, Walker lamented how Celie lost her childhood innocence because of the lynching of her biological father by white townspeople, her mother's tragic illness, and the abduction at birth of her children, who—as Walker wrote—might have been murdered by "the rapist psychopath who claims to be her father." Whatever ugliness we see in Celie is a lie created by those individuals and institutions bent on degrading her and by her decades of enduring drudgery and abuse.

Almost forty years after she first gave us Celie, Walker tells me, "Here's the most amazing thing about the issue of Celie's ugliness. Given everything that her stepfather did to abuse her, everybody believed him." She continues, "They believe him when he says that she's nearly twenty, though she's fourteen. They believe him when he says she's ugly. They believe him, the reader believes everything. I'm always shocked by it. I'm always thinking, 'Well, but you see the liar.'"

A few years ago, Erivo and I both presented at the 2017 MAKERS Conference, themed #BeBold, in Southern California. Despite having won the 2016 Tony Award for Best Actress in a Musical and a 2017 Grammy Award for Best Musical Theater Album, Erivo at first was reluctant to sing "I Am Here," Celie's stirring solo, before our live audience. "I tried very hard not to do this song after I did it four hundred and ninety-eight times, eight shows a week, six days a week," she told us. Standing in a sexy black tank top with her toned forearms and platinum-blonde waves, Erivo actively distinguished herself from the muted modest clothing and plaited hairstyle that she wore while playing Celie onstage. "And I guess I resist the song a lot now because in order to get to the place to sing the song I had to live inside a character that was shoved around stage and called 'ugly' for two or three hours."

She confessed, "And you think, 'She's playing a character and she'll be fine.' But, after time three fifty, three sixty, four hundred—it starts to wear on the skin a bit and the person inside the character starts to hear it for real. So, imagine eight shows a week and hearing the word 'ugly.' And imagine the only way I could get to this point to sing the song is to go through that. So, I resisted.

But I guess its message is more important than its circumstances." And then, with all her might, she belted out the opening line, "I don't need you to love me."

Alice turns quiet when I tell her of Erivo's reticence. "That has always bugged me, that the person who plays her has that question because they don't want to be considered ugly," she divulges. "What I'm trying to tell them is that these are all the reasons why she is beautiful too. She's like her sister. Like my grandmother Rachel upon whom she's based somewhat, I really regret that the character, the person playing that role, had to bear the representation that others put on her and Celie." I was struck by how much Alice was not only describing this novel but commentating on her own hopefulness, a writerly trait of hers that has always distinguished her from other authors. Her fiction imagines a better possible world, and then by showing that the self-realization and social acceptance of her characters are possible, it guides others so that we can achieve it on our own. So, even though the real-life Rachel, who throughout Walker's childhood and until her death remained chained to a life of drudgery and violence, never achieved the fictional Celie's arc of self-realization and social acceptance, Walker's wish for another ending for her grandmother's fate actually changed the lives of the many of us who've come of age reading her work.

When Rachel Little was a timid teenager, her father forced her to join the Walker family. She was neither Alice Walker's paternal grandfather Henry Clay Walker's first or even third choice as a spouse. She was there as a result of desperation. Henry, born in 1888 to Sallie Montgomery and Albert Walker, grew up well to do as the son of one of the few African American cotton farmers in Putnam County, Georgia, who tilled his own land. Henry's father, Albert, after whom Alice Walker famously named Celie's husband, was so well off that he earned the envy of his white neighbors until a boll weevil infestation permanently ruined their family crop. Even though his family quickly fell in social ranking, Albert maintained an air of superiority over black people in Eatonton. Meanwhile, his son, Henry, took up with Estella Perry, a gorgeous, freethinking young woman nicknamed "Shug" who frequented bars and juke joints. Given her sullied reputation, Albert forbade his son from marrying Shug and forced him to wed Kate Nelson, a nearby churchgoing woman whom Henry never loved nor grew to desire. Rather than give up Shug, Henry simply kept up their trysts, covering up his inability to stand up to his father and the emasculating effects of Jim Crow by excessively drinking, once even chasing his wife, Kate, through the fields, and "shooting at her; missing only because he was drunk."

Over time, Kate refused to submit to either Henry's infidelities or his fists. And for a few short weeks, she took on a lover of her own. "She'd been putting up with Pa-Pa's affair for all those years," Ruth, Alice Walker's older sister, told her sibling's biographer, Evelyn White, about their grandmother. "So, I guess she looked at the situation and said, 'Well, two can play this game.'" But this release was fleeting. When Kate eventually called off the relationship, her lover refused. On July 4, 1921, a month shy of her thirtieth birthday, he ambushed her on her walk home from church. Aiming a gun at her chest, he shot her in front of her son, Willie Lee Walker, who fell down on his blood-soaked knees to cradle his mother. She died the next day.

Willie Lee could never recover from his mother's death and never forgave his father for getting married a month after Kate's death to Rachel, a teenage girl who was only a few years older than Willie Lee was. Having only a couple of days to mourn before meeting his father's child bride, Willie Lee refused to treat her with anything other than begrudging respect, and never called her by any name other than "Miss Rachel" for the rest of his life. In time, he'd learn to stuff those feelings of rage deep, deep down inside, eventually taking it out on his children, including his own wife and Alice's mother, Minnie Lou. So Alice grew up hearing only parts of Rachel's story, learning bits and pieces of her biography in conversations that she overheard. In her essay "Writing *The Color Purple*," she recounted the experience of hiking with her sister one day that sparked the novel's plot. Though Walker didn't disclose the names of Rachel and Shug at the time, she writes that she and her sister began discussing a lover's triangle in their family in which two women not only felt married to the same man but were so close that they even shared silk panties with each other. Tickled by how pragmatic their intimacy had become, Alice grew obsessed with the women, a fascination that stayed with her for years, through several moves, trips abroad, illnesses, a divorce, and "all kinds of heartaches and revelations." Eventually, those female figures took over her life and moved to the center of the novel that she was creating, bit by bit, in her head.

Later on, those family rumors became her plot points. With all the victims and villains dead, Walker had only gossip and girlhood memory upon which to rely. According to Walker's sister, Ruth, who was only five years old when Shug Perry visited Putnam County, Georgia, in the mid-1940s, she, Rachel, and Shug ran across the fields one Sunday afternoon after church to use the bathroom at the outhouse. "You see, my grandmother never had any of those soft, frilly things," Ruth said of Shug's pink silk underpants. "Knowing how Pa-Pa abused her, Miss Shug, maybe out of guilt, but mostly out of kindness, tried to make up for some of the hardships in Ma-Ma's life." Not only did Shug give her those panties right then and there but she continued to send lingerie and other clothes of comfort to Rachel over the years.

Rachel's granddaughters never knew what Rachel did with those gifts other than keep them out of her husband's way. In those years, Henry Clay softened. Not because of Rachel, but because of Shug. Though her main residence was in Cleveland, Shug took up with Henry on her return trips home, eventually having two children with him despite his marriages to Kate and then Rachel.

"In the beginning, this was hard on my grandmother because she essentially had 'the other woman' under her roof," Ruth reflected. But, as time went by, Henry, eternally in love with Shug, began to treat Rachel differently, even better. "Ma-Ma made peace with the situation. Eventually she and Miss Shug became good friends." But rather than focusing on the tenderness between Rachel and Shug, Alice saw the oppression in her stepgrandmother's life. "What I remember about her is how little voice she had. I don't know what she thought in those days and months and years when she was silent," Walker, wiping tears from her face, quietly tells me. "I wondered about her thoughts because my work is fiction and I thought it was high time she had a voice."

Born on February 9, 1944, Alice Malsenior Walker was the youngest of eight children. Her father and mother, Willie Lee Walker and Minnie Tallulah Grant Walker were both sharecroppers, with Minnie also working as a domestic. There was trauma on the other side of Alice's family as well. Her maternal grandfather, William A. Grant, was a languid, obstinate, light-skinned man saddled with debt and twelve children who took his disappointments out on his children, including his daughter Minnie Lou and his wife, Nettie, his anger increasing with each of Nettie's pregnancies. Writing about Nettie, after whom she'd later name Celie's sister, Walker said, "She was loving and kind. Though never with sufficient energy or time to leave the house and environs." Reflecting back on her ancestors, Walker once wrote, "Approaching my mid-fifties, I allowed myself to feel deeply the tragedy of all their lives, but especially the lives of my grandmothers who might have been adventurous, creative, fascinating women, if they had been allowed freedom to thrive."

Ninety miles west of Eatonton is the cul-de-sac where my own maternal grandmother, Luretha Lee Griffin, died. After she moved there from New Jersey with her youngest daughter about fifteen years ago, I rarely saw her. Permanently paralyzed at age fifty-five by a stroke that I had witnessed, my grandmother always seemed so stoic, breaking her silence only to pray for and over me. Luretha, born on October 26, 1925, was the first and only child of Martha Jane and John Little, and grew up in Greenville, North Carolina, a Tar Heel town that owed its fortune to trains and tobacco. It'd take almost twenty years after *Brown v. Board of Education* for the Pitt County public schools to be legally integrated. By then, Luretha had stopped going home. She'd married James Stewart Howell in 1946, only to find him to be a godless man who constantly beat her and their two sons. Finding no respite from his abuse, she left their house in Virginia and moved to Brooklyn without her sons, a decision for which they never forgave her. My aunt tells me this as we sit in a local seafood restaurant, only to later text me a black-and-white picture of her older brothers, James and William, as toddlers with their young mother, Luretha, holding her crawling children. Age twenty-four, wearing a black wool coat and ribbon bonnet, she was so vibrant and eager that she is unrecognizable to me. And being so close to Walker's birthplace reminds me that this male violence crosses generations and ends up sticking to us granddaughters and shaping many things, even our prose.

Alice *chose* to see her grandmother Rachel. And by doing so, she did something even more remarkable: she put black women at the center of America's epic history. By shuttling between the suffrage and early desegregation movements that backdrop Celie's life *and* the severe post-1960s backlash to feminism and civil rights that greeted the novel upon its arrival in the Reagan era, Walker told the story of racial inequality and women's rights through the life of an African American woman, a story too often absent in the historical record. As such, she reimagined the arc of the women's movement itself, birthing a new generation of feminist writers, artists, and activists for whom reading Celie's letters was a fundamental rite of passage.

"All the women on the planet who just live these lives of drudgery and rape, battering and overwork," Alice says to me. "They die finally and people thinking back over their lives can't even remember a conversation. And really, what does she think? All these people who've been silenced. So that's part of why I gave her a voice. I said, okay. You know you learn to write. Learn to read. And then just tell your story in your language. And let the chips fall where they may."

In her 1972 essay, "In Search of Our Mothers' Gardens," a decade before the publication of *The Color Purple*, Alice mourned how year after year, century after century, creative black women who might have been painters, sculptors, and writers were not simply denied a room of their own: under slavery, the very act of reading and writing had been criminalized. If they were lucky, these artists turned to other forms of self-expression, like cooking, quilting, or gardening, outside the purview of their oppressors; but more often than not, these women were driven mad. "What did it mean for a black woman to be an artist in our grandmothers' time? In our great-grandmothers' day?" Alice had queried. What did it mean for Walker's grandmothers? For mine? "The answer," Walker calculated, "was cruel enough to stop the blood."

Three months after I met Walker, I was in Atlanta to present at the National Women's Studies Association conference. I had a few free hours, so I decided to revisit her archives at Emory's Stuart A. Rose Manuscript, Archives, and Rare Book Library.

There, among the hundreds of images, was only one with the name Rachel. When I requested it, I half expected to see a grinning Whoopi Goldberg looking back at me—so memorable was her performance from the film version. Instead, I cradled in my hand a three-by-five black-and-white picture of four women.

Written on the back of the photo in pen were four names:

Aunt Minnie Lou
? Miss Mary
Miss Rachel
Grandma

I tried to match their names to their faces. The next day, I excitedly texted the picture to Walker. It was late and I knew that she had just spent hours in Atlanta in a packed auditorium in a public conversation with Beverly Guy-Sheftall, so I assumed she'd either be too tired to respond or was on her way back to California. At first, her response to my fact-finding mission was to be as helpful and instructive as possible. She told me that the teenage girl looking at me with folded hands and a slight lean was Minnie Lou, who eventually became Walker's mother. Next to her was Miss Mary, a dark-brown-skinned family friend of above-average height. And then she simply texted "Grandmother," referring to the next two women. I was confused. Which grandmother? Who was Miss Rachel? A family friend? Or her grandmother too? Bewildered, I texted her again to gain more clarity. But once I boarded my flight and had no Wi-Fi, I lost my connection to Alice and her past.

Staring at the picture as I sat on the plane, I searched her grandmothers' faces for recognition. I assumed the stout figure with the wide-brimmed hat was her maternal grandmother, Nettie Lou. But a woman in a black dress and white shoes stood out among the others, who were wearing white dresses and black flats. Miss Rachel, with braids and a polka-dot ruffled frock, had the softest expression on her oval face, her almond complexion akin to that of another woman of her era, the famous dancer and chanteuse Josephine Baker. The image was far closer to the 1981 sketch of Celie in Alice's journal that she texted me after we first met:

> *Being skinny is Celie's major fault. Since when one is a woman & very skinny (with tiny breasts) one's form was not considered womanly. Hence Mr. ____'s frequent reminder to Celie that "you shape(d) funny." Today we would say Celie has a model's figure. Her other "ugliness" consists of a furtive, beaten down manner, & unkempt*

hair & clothing (she had no one to teach her to care for herself). As she begins to create herself through her writing, her love of Shug & Nettie, she begins to take on an outer beauty that approximates the extraordinary loveliness of her spirit.

As I looked at Rachel again and again, I was a bit ashamed, but mostly transfixed by my own error. I had not believed in her beauty either. I assumed that when Walker was embellishing her loveliness, she was trying to make up for Rachel's pain by attempting to convince me of her innate beauty. But *I* was the problem because I had chosen not to *see* Rachel.

When I landed in Newark near midnight, my phone vibrated with a new message that Alice must have sent to me while I was in midair. She wrote me a short note that instantly reshaped the prism through which I saw Rachel and, as a result, how I would teach Celie's character going forward. "This was before her hardest years with my grandfather," Walker texted about Rachel. As I stood in the quiet airport, Alice's words bouncing off my bright screen offset my wave of exhaustion.

"She was really the best looking of all," she wrote. "They couldn't see that then."

Minnie Lou Walker, Miss Mary Little, Rachel Little
(Celie) and Grandmother Nettie Lee Grant

2. I HAD TO DO A LOT OF OTHER WRITING TO GET TO THIS POINT

IT WOULD TAKE Alice Walker six books and two decades before she put her grandmother's voice at the center of a story. But, as early as 1966, she'd already begun to reimagine her grandfather Henry Clay through Grange Copeland, a Georgia sharecropper and the titular character of her debut novel, an exploration of the impact of domestic violence on three generations of African Americans. Nearing her twenty-second birthday, Walker, sitting in a dimly lit, damp apartment in New York City's East Village, had decided to return to the South. And rather than plot the novel in the middle of the civil rights movement that she actively was a part of, Walker set the opening of *The Third Life of Grange Copeland* thirty years before.

I read *Third Life* on my own in college. I picked it up after taking a freshman seminar on women writers in which we read Walker's short story "Everyday Use," about a newly college-educated black woman who returns to her mother in the rural South in the late 1960s. In her pretentiousness, racial dogma, and perfectly coiffed Afro, I saw my own contradictions and newly found identity politics. Shortly after reading *Third Life*, my seventeen-year-old self went around proclaiming to my friends that this was by far her best novel. While I was still new to the ways of feminism, my racial instincts were sharper and more clearly defined. As I was a child of the Black Power movement, my Afro-wearing Trinidadian father, Lenny, and my African American mother, Volora, who was thirteen years his junior, bestowed me with a first name that encapsulated their own cultural pride while also staying in step with the 1970s trend of black parents turning to African languages or Arabic when naming their children. My name is a combination of *salam*, the Arabic word meaning peace, as in the Islamic greeting *As-salamu alaykum*, "Peace be upon you"; *shah*, the Farsi for king or leader, which always made me stand out; and the middle syllable *mi*, which my parents interpreted as black. So they pulled from various cultures and languages to invent my name, making both me and it quintessentially African American. Growing up with such a strong racial consciousness made me more sympathetic to those black people who put issues of racism ahead of those of sexism, and narratives of black male vulnerability at the hands of white police officers over those of black women at the hands of white and black men. Because Walker so clearly incriminated the white landowners who forced black families into sharecropping in *Third Life*, while she also so clearly redeemed Grange at the novel's end, I found it an easier book to praise and defend because I thought it would be impossible for my black men friends to say that either Walker or I hated them.

Speculating almost thirty years after the publication of *Third Life* on what compelled her to write an African American novel about domestic violence during the height of the civil rights movement, Walker wrote, "It was an incredibly difficult novel to write, for I had to look at, and name, and speak up about violence among black people in the black community." She wondered, "At the same time that all black people (and some whites)—including me and my family—were enduring massive psychological and physical violence from white supremacists in Southern states, why write such a novel?"

The most influential narratives of the 1960s, such as Claude Brown's novel *Manchild in the Promised Land*, Amiri Baraka's music criticism *Blues People*, and James Baldwin's *The Fire Next Time* and short story collection *Going to Meet the Man*, depicted racism as a problem that primarily impacted black men. The work that overshadowed all others and was most formative for me, however, was *The Autobiography of Malcolm X*, a breathtaking memoir as told to Alex Haley that detailed Malcolm's political consciousness, religious awakening, and confrontation with American racism. Canceled by Doubleday three weeks after Malcolm's assassination in 1965, it was published later that year by Grove Press and sold millions of copies, becoming the most influential African American autobiography for half a century.

Growing up in segregated Georgia, Alice was intimately familiar with the ways of racists. She carried that burden with her when she boarded a silver-and-blue Greyhound bus destined for Spelman College in Atlanta in August 1961, along with three gifts—a suitcase, a sewing machine, and a typewriter—that her mother, Minnie Lou, had bought for her while earning less than twenty dollars a week as a domestic. Alone, on her way to a new city, Walker sat down in the front section designated "for whites only," and at first refused the white bus driver's command for her to sit in the "colored section" of the bus. Eventually she relented, though she later recalled, "I knew he had not seen the last of me. In those seconds of moving, everything changed. I was eager to bring an end to the South that permitted my humiliation."

Once on campus, Walker found herself drawn to those Spelman students and to Howard Zinn, their thirty-nine-year-old Jewish-American faculty adviser and American history professor, who taught at Spelman from 1956 to 1963. In his article "Finishing School for Pickets," published in *The Nation* in August 1960, Zinn praised a dormitory notice on campus that encouraged Spelmanites to protest: "Young Ladies Who Can Picket, Please Sign Below." Zinn not only inspired and encouraged his students to be activists but also joined them in their sit-in at the white section of the gallery at the Georgia State Capitol in January 1961. When Alice enrolled in Revolution and Response, Zinn's Russian history course, she was determined to put her unique stamp on everything she encountered there, even the works of Dostoyevsky and Tolstoy. Zinn wrote in his memoir of her work, "Not only had I never read a paper by an undergraduate with such critical intelligence, but I had rarely read a literary essay of such grace and style by anyone. And she was nineteen, from a family farm in Eatonton, Georgia."

Inside and outside the classroom, Zinn's progressive politics were rare on Spelman's traditional campus. He nurtured safe space for students like Alice to be politically curious and active. He served as an adviser to the Student Nonviolent Coordinating Committee (SNCC), and his increasing involvement in the civil rights movements soon angered Albert Manley, Spelman's first African American president, who felt that Zinn was revolutionizing Spelman students. Despite Zinn's tenure, in 1963 Manley relieved Zinn of his duties with the college. Later reflecting on his dismissal in his memoir *You Can't Be Neutral on a Moving Train*, Zinn wrote, "President Manley was adamant. To visiting delegations, he gave the reason he had not put in the letter. That I was insubordinate." He recalled, "It was true, I suppose." Students campaigned to have Zinn remain at Spelman, with Walker even publishing a letter to the editor of Spelman's newspaper, *The Spotlight*, to decry its lack of freedom of expression. Zinn's discharge was a significant loss for the campus and for Walker herself. The civil rights movement was growing outside of Spelman's gates, and Walker felt she had no choice but to join. "There is nothing really here for me," she said of Spelman. "It is almost like being buried alive."

With the help of faculty member Staughton Lynd, Walker transferred to Sarah Lawrence, the predominantly white women's liberal arts college in Bronxville, New York, in early 1964. While studying there, she published her first short story and learned to feel that what she thought "had some meaning." At home intellectually, Alice soon felt another alienation as one of the few black women on campus. While she sought connection with those other few, Alice also sought an even deeper connection to her identity by traveling to the newly decolonized countries of Kenya, Tanzania, and Uganda the summer before her senior year. Touring East Africa with the Experiment in International Living, a Vermont-based summer immersion program, Alice was saddened and shocked by the depth of poverty that surrounded her on her travels. "The colonizers had pillaged the land and poisoned the culture," she later told her biographer, Evelyn White. "Of course, I was happy to be in Africa, to connect with my roots and to see the people still fighting for survival. But, it was very hard."

In Uganda, Alice visited the countryside. While there Alice received an unexpected visit from David DeMoss, a white Peace Corps volunteer in Tanzania and former boyfriend from college.

It did not take long for them to rekindle their earlier passion, despite the fact that neither of them traveled with contraception and Alice had left behind her newly acquired birth control pills in the States. "So, caught up in the joy of the moment, we made love," Walker told White. "I knew immediately I was pregnant." Back at Sarah Lawrence that fall, her fears were confirmed. Her pregnancy immediately made her anxious that she would have to drop out of college. She felt afraid to tell her devoutly religious parents. Adding more stress was Walker's inability in those pre–*Roe v. Wade* days to find a doctor who would perform an abortion for her. With each passing day, Alice's depression set in. She began planning her suicide and even started to sleep with a razor under her pillow.

Eventually, Alice's friends from Sarah Lawrence, especially Carole Darden, one of the few black women on campus with Walker, contributed funds to ensure that Alice could safely terminate her pregnancy. Alice would go on to fictionalize her experience in "Abortion," a short story that appeared in *You Can't Keep a Good Woman Down* and later in her second novel, *Meridian*. In the former, a young married woman named Imani flies to New York to have her second abortion; the first took place during college, this one after a few years of marriage to Clarence, and having already given birth to her now toddler daughter, Clarice. En route to the Margaret Sanger clinic in Greenwich Village, Imani, pulling from Walker's own actual experiences, frequently remembers her first abortion "as wonderful, bearing as it had all the marks of a supreme coming of age and a seizing of the direction of her own life, as well as a comprehension of existence that never left her: that life—what one saw about one and called Life—was not a facade." But after that brief moment of nostalgia, Imani also recalled that she "hemorrhaged steadily for six weeks, and was not well again for a year."

During her final semester at Sarah Lawrence, while Walker avoided writing on the subject of abortion, she did write poems that reflected on her life in the South, her suicidal thoughts, and her trip to East Africa. Right before she graduated in January 1966, Walker shared them with her writing professor and mentor, Muriel Rukeyser, bravely slipping them underneath Rukeyser's office door one night. Rukeyser passed them on to her own literary agent, Monica McCall, who placed the book with an editor at Harcourt Brace Jovanovich. Three years later, this loose collection of poems became her debut book, *Once*.

After graduation, Alice intended to return to Africa as a writer, this time to Senegal, but then she came across an article about the entrenched white resistance to the civil rights movement in the United States. She'd later recall that she couldn't help but ask, "What was the point of studying French in Senegal? When black parents in Biloxi and Tuskegee couldn't vote, when their children were given secondhand books (if any) from white schools inscribed with 'Nigger' and 'Long Live the Klan'?" So instead of going to Senegal, Walker bought a one-way ticket to Mississippi and took a job with the NAACP Legal Defense and Educational Fund, where she put her typewriter to good use and traveled to Greenwood, a community about five hours west of Atlanta, to document the lives of black sharecroppers, men and women as familiar to her as her parents, who had been forced out of their homes after trying to register to vote.

While in Greenwood, Walker worked with Melvyn (Mel)

Rosenman Leventhal, a white, Jewish American law student from New York. They often traveled together, and their work and friendship drew animosity, even violent threats from local whites who saw any consensual relationship between a black woman and a white man as an affront to their southern racial order. Alice later recalled a man coming up to her at a motel where she was staying—a place that hadn't been deemed safe for a black woman, let alone one with a white man—and warning her, "Don't you let the sun go down on you in this town here." ("Such a cliché," she noted.)

But the dangers were real. Only two summers before, three activists—James Chaney, Andrew Goodman, and Michael Schwerner, the latter two from New York City—were murdered only a few hours from Greenwood. In the summer of 1966, Alice and Mel's admiration and respect for each other's courage, commitment, and compassion transformed into attraction and abiding love.

After graduating from NYU School of Law in 1967, Mel and Alice married in New York City before moving to Jackson, where Mel began his law practice. They were the first legally married interracial couple in the state of Mississippi. Two years later, when Alice gave birth to Rebecca their only child together, the fact that they were risking not just their own lives but also Rebecca's by openly defying the strict color line upon which Mississippi prided itself was to take a huge toll on their marriage.

White supremacy hovers over all of Grange's interactions with his family and community in Walker's first novel, *Third Life*, but racism was not the only topic about which Walker felt compelled to write. Responding to her own query about why she felt obligated to reckon with the internal family dynamics of a rural black patriarch, Walker, in her 1988 afterword to *Third Life*, wrote, "The simplest answer is, perhaps, that I could not help it." There is a moment in *Third Life* that is so devastating that it is always the first scene I remember when I think of this novel. Near the end of the book, Grange's only son, Brownfield, kills his wife, Mem, with a shotgun in front of their children. As a result of witnessing this tragedy, their youngest daughter, Ruth, is so overtaken with nausea and numbness that she can only gaze at her dying mother, who lay "faceless among a scattering of gravel in a pool of blood, in which were scattered around her head like a halo, a dozen bright yellow oranges that glistened on one side from the light." Partly based on Walker's father watching his mother's murder right before him, this image also came from Walker's own memory of seeing the body of her dead neighbor in the funeral home. "I described in the novel exactly as she appeared to me then."

As a teenager, Alice often babysat for a family that lived next door to a local funeral parlor where her older sister worked as a beautician and cosmetologist. One day, while visiting the funeral parlor, Alice walked into a room where a woman lay stretched out on a white metal table, her head resting on an iron pillow. She'd been shot in the face by her husband. "Writing about it years later was the only way I could be free of such a powerful and despairing image," she concluded.

In *Third Life*, Mem's death was the book's climax and emotional center: Brownfield's murder of Mem prompts his father's own redemption. Grange, who abandoned his son and his wife, Margaret, and avoided his sharecropping debt by moving up north, has a "third life" when he takes care of his granddaughter Ruth. Aware that his paternal gesture neither absolves the terror he inflicted on his son nor alleviates Brownfield's hatred of him, Grange finds solace and redemption in his relationship with Ruth. In the final scene of the book, he gives up his life to defend her from a vengeful Brownfield, who tries to shoot his daughter and kills Grange instead.

And because that woman, lying cold in the funeral home, shared the same tragic ending as Alice's own paternal grandmother, Kate, she could not help but think about her own family. "Its roots always seemed to be embedded in my father's need to dominate my mother and their children," Walker surmised. "And in her resistance (and ours), verbal and physical, to any such domination." Fueling *Third Life* was Walker's realization that it was not just Mrs. Walker or Alice's grandmother; such violence doomed the fate of all women. That is why she named Ruth's mother Mem, after the French *la même*, which in English means "the same."

Most critical responses to *Grange* were positive. *Kirkus Reviews* described it as "a harrowingly detailed family saga spanning three generations." Likewise, Kay Bourne, a journalist for the Boston-based *Bay State Banner*, picked up on the novel's unique storytelling: "*Third Life of Grange Copeland* is more personal than the historical novel form." She concluded, "Most poignant is the relation of the lives of black women, who were ready and strong and trusted, only to so often be abused by the conditions of their oppressed lives and the misdirected anger of their men." Though Victor A. Kramer, an English professor at Georgia State University, considered this plot of intergenerational men's hatred of women "near fantasy" in his review for *Library Journal*, he also appreciated that "Walker's characters are not pretty ones. Yet this is the point: dignity can be maintained amidst intense degradation."

In a flippant appraisal for *Saturday Review*, however, the critic Josephine Hendin accused Walker of depicting Brownfield as "a murderous, whining beast." Walker's sympathy, Hendin suggested, was with his wife and with all black women whom Walker saw as victims of both white racism and black men's rage. Because of that, Hendin sniped, "Brownfield appears to have an intense self-hatred; to him black is anything but beautiful. Miss Walker hates his self-hatred too much to dissect it." Writing directly to the newspaper, Walker retorted, "Can Josephine Hendin really express such mid-Reconstruction condescension and be taken seriously . . . ? And if she can be, then all those tears allegedly shed for us 'quietly suffering blacks' have been misdirected." Saving her biggest rebuttal for Hendin's accusation that Grange "lost his self-loathing" by beating up as many white people as possible, Walker blasted that "what motivates the old man to change is love of self (not love or hatred of white folks—because to him as to me, white folks are mainly irrelevant unless they are standing directly in one's sunlight; which, of course, they too often are)."

Walker was not concerned with Hendin's misreading of her intent—whether or not Grange's redemption was convincing or fulfilling enough; she was suspicious of any reviewer, white or black, who dictated the terms upon which a black writer could express her imagination. Undeterred, Walker continued to center the lives and perspectives of everyday southern black women in subsequent books: the short story collections *You Can't Keep a Good Woman Down* (1971) and *In Love & Trouble: Stories of Black Women* (1973), and in her second book of poetry, *Revolutionary Petunias & Other Poems* (1973). As she traversed forms, she was steadfastly committed to establishing her voice as a southern, black, woman writer, who with each publication cultivated a loyal readership and, over time, fellowship with other black women writers.

When Toni Morrison released *Sula* in 1973, Walker and June Jordan had yet to found "The Sisterhood," a collective of black women writers in New York City, which also included Morrison, the playwright Ntozake Shange, and the journalist Audrey Edwards. But when Alice read the scathing review of *Sula* in the pages of the *New York Times* that December, she became incensed. Praising Morrison's skill at characterization, the *Times'* Sara Blackburn wrote, "Like the gorgeous characters of Garcia Marquez, they have a heroic quality, and it's hard to believe we haven't known them forever." But such praise was halfhearted. Urging Morrison to reach beyond "the black side of provincial American life," Blackburn suggested "that she might easily transcend the early and unintentionally limiting classification 'black woman writer' and take her place among the most serious, important and talented American novelists now working."

Angered by Blackburn's assumptions, Walker offered a riposte that appeared the next month in the *Times*: "As I read over Ms. Blackburn's review I began to discern why, as a reviewer, she seems so utterly untrustworthy." Walker concluded, "It is because she, like only too many reviewers before her, is incapable apparently of experiencing black fiction as art but must read it instead as sociology." Walker's insistence that the black writer be not only a recorder of African American social ills but also a creator who chooses to chronicle black life resembled her earlier disregard for Hendin's dismissal of *Third Life*. But her defense was also a hint of what was to come. By the end of the decade, Walker had gained as much editorial control of her work as possible. But first she had to return to the college at which she became a writer.

Meridian is a difficult book. Or at least that's what I thought as a college junior as I struggled with the novel. The main character of the novel, originally published in 1976, is Meridian Hill, a young woman who leaves the suffocating and conservative environment of the all-black women's college Saxon (based on Spelman) to join the civil rights movement. She becomes romantically involved with a fellow activist named Truman Held, with whom she has a tumultuous on-and-off relationship, and becomes pregnant by him. Like Alice, Meridian has an illegal abortion. However, Walker also wanted to tell an even bigger story of black women's reproductive oppression. When Meridian elects to terminate her pregnancy, the doctor racially stereotypes her as irresponsible and unfit for motherhood, and decides to sterilize her without her knowledge or consent.

Walker started work on the novel while she lived in Mississippi, and *Meridian* is as much a book about the aftermath of the civil rights movement in which she was intimately involved as it is about the dissolution of romantic relationships, particularly interracial ones that were born out of that racial struggle. By the time Walker and Leventhal left Mississippi for good in 1975, their eight-year marriage had suffered deeply under the daily strain of living together in the segregated South. When *Meridian* came out a year later, Alice and Mel's differences were irreconcilable; they soon divorced.

In the novel, Walker explores another interracial dynamic—one that was much more common in the period though equally as dangerous as her own—that of a black man and a white woman. Through Truman's marriage to Lynne, a white Jewish civil rights worker from the suburbs who moves to Mississippi because she believes that "the black people of the South were Art," Walker told another story of the costs and consequences of having one's interracial child grow up in the civil rights movement. After the rape and murder of their young daughter, Camara, Truman abandons Lynne and goes searching for Meridian. Later, as Lynne is raped by a former friend, Tommy Odds, she pictures herself inside "a racist painting she had once seen in *Esquire* of a nude white woman surrounded by black men." The novel ends with Truman, after several unsuccessful attempts to achieve personal and financial success and to stay married to Lynne after the death of their daughter, returning to the South. He goes there to continue Meridian's activism, and takes on her legacy of remaining in the South to fight for racial equality long after all their fellow civil rights workers have moved on.

While the love triangle of Meridian, Lynne, and Truman partly anticipates that of Celie, Shug, and Albert, it was also allegorical, a story of a people on the verge of freedom. "Both ruthless and tender," the critic Margo Jefferson wrote, praising the novel in *Newsweek*. "Walker documents the turning toward radical violence in the movement: the wearing psychological and sexual confrontations between black and white co-workers that often revealed them to be as much enemies as comrades." And while these internecine battles took on a very different form in *The Color Purple*, it seemed to some readers that violence against black women was a major theme in her work. So much so that in 1983, in his *New York Times* review of *The Color Purple*, the writer Mel Watkins noted, "In *Meridian*, however, the friction between black men and women is merely one of several themes; in *The Color Purple* the role of male domination in the frustration of black women's struggle for independence is clearly the focus."

Most important, it was with *Meridian* that Walker began to take full control over all the stages of her writing: from first draft to final copy. She later admitted to *Newsweek* that before writing her "happiest book" (*The Color Purple*), she had "to do all the other writing to get to this point" and fight to be a black artist who was censored by neither white nor black critics. After being entirely unimpressed with her Harcourt editor, Tony Godwin, whom she inherited after her original editor, Hiram Haydn, died in 1973, Walker decided that after her experience publishing *Meridian* with him, she'd only send her editors a completed manuscript. "Generations of people have suffered and died so that I could be this free," Alice told her biographer, Evelyn White. "And with that always in my heart, I write whatever I feel needs to be written. I work for the ancestors. Period."

It did not take long for those ancestors to assume the form of Celie, Shug, and Sofia and to want to be the authors of their own story. On a warm spring day in 1980 in Walker's Brooklyn living room, they rushed to find her, and with her green pen she began to write:

> *You better never tell no one but god. It'd kill your mammy.*
> *Dear God,*
> *I am fourteen years old. I am I have always been a good*
> *girl. Maybe you can give me a sign letting me know what is*
> *happening to me.*

By June of the following year, Alice had finished the novel. But she had to wait for more words to come to her. And to make that happen, she sold her house, left her job, and set out for San Francisco with Rebecca. Then they moved even farther north to find the right country house, a one-bedroom cottage in Boonville with an apple orchard as backyard.

Finally, Alice had found a place where her characters felt safe enough to open up their entire world for her.

3. IN THIS STRUGGLE
LANGUAGE IS CRUCIAL

"DEAR ALICE," typed John Ferrone, Walker's third editor at Harcourt Brace Jovanovich, in a letter dated September 9, 1981. "Now that Wendy has tracked you down, I feel I can write you *somewhere*. I just want to say a few things about *The Color Purple* and perhaps start you thinking again."

Aware of Walker's hard-fought autonomy, Ferrone hesitated before constructing his next sentence.

"First, language."

Assuring her that her choice to write the novel from the point of view of a rural, African American girl named Celie was not an "impediment" (as she feared in a letter that she wrote to him a few months earlier), Ferrone committed to publishing her entire novel "without changing a word." But he was concerned that the vitality of Celie's voice came at the expense of Nettie's, who was an educated Christian missionary in West Africa. "You say *you* want the reader to get restless with Nettie's white English. Alice, we know what white English sounds like," he protested. "(It's a marvelous language, too)." Finding Nettie's tone to be overly didactic, he wanted Walker to set up a bigger contrast between these characters' linguistic styles as well as abandon her most innovative strategy yet: the epistolary conceit. Alice thought that Ferrone's feedback, which also suggested changing the book's title (he found *The Color Purple* "too abstract for the kind of story you're telling"), was a result of his own bias against Celie's voice. Walker pushed back. "Here is the *least* that can be said," she wrote. She was, of course, quite happy with her violaceous title and felt that the letter writing between the two sisters was central to her story, for it was also "making a comment about how women's writing occurred in the past." But her larger point, the one upon which she ended up hanging her entire novel and career, was that Celie's speech was not just equal to Nettie's but rather superior to it.

The manuscript that Ferrone read was quite close to the original, which she'd started in her personal journal and finished in her yellow notepad the year before. Opening with Celie, orphaned by age fourteen, writing letters to God, *The Color Purple* is the story of her sexual trauma and gradual triumph as she redefines her relationship to her abuse, her sexuality, her literacy, and God. Celie's awakening is prompted by her abusive stepfather, Alphonso, whom she calls "Pa." He warns her not to tell anybody but "God" after he rapes her, twice impregnates her, and takes both babies, Adam and Olivia, away, after leaving her to believe that he killed them both. Shortly thereafter, when a neighboring widower, Mr. _____ (whose name we later learn is Albert), approaches him about marrying Nettie, Pa instantly refuses and offers Celie instead, thus forcing her into a marriage marred by domestic violence, and making her a teenage stepmother to Albert's four children. Fleeing abuse from Pa, Nettie briefly lives with Celie, only to leave again because of Albert's harassment of her.

Once Celie is separated from her sister, she forges a sisterhood with the defiant Sofia, who marries Albert's son Harpo after becoming pregnant, and also falls in love with the glamorous and free-spirited Shug Avery, a blues singer and Albert's former lover. When Shug reveals to Celie that Albert has been hiding Nettie's letters during Nettie's time as a missionary in Liberia, Celie has another awakening, begins to title her letters "Dear Nettie," and leaves Albert for Shug. In the final chapters of the book, Celie moves into a house that she inherited from her biological parents, successfully opens her own pants shop, and thanks to Shug's and a redeemed Albert's efforts is able to reconnect with Nettie and her children, Olivia and Adam, after thirty years. Celie begins her last letter "Dear stars, dear trees, dear sky, dear peoples. Dear Everything. Dear God," and embarks on this next phase of her journey with Shug and their blended family in communion with Nature.

To tell Celie's epic tale, Walker broke multiple taboos. The first was that of incest. When we first encounter Celie's own private thoughts to herself, we believe, as she does, that "Pa" is her actual father and only learn much later in the novel that a white mob lynched her real father. Without that knowledge, *The Color Purple* first appears to be an incest story. And while Walker was not the first African American novelist to capture that horror, she was the only one at that time to capture this violation from the point of view of the rape victim. Both Ralph Ellison's 1952 best-selling *Invisible Man* and Toni Morrison's 1970 debut, *The Bluest Eye*, depicted the actual scene of father-daughter sexual abuse through the eyes of the fathers. Unlike Ellison's novel, whose sympathetic portrayal of the assailant risked turning him into a southern folk hero, both Morrison's and Walker's novels maintained a narrative empathy for their girl victims. However, Walker begins our entire reading experience with the moment of violation and in such vivid detail that she not only subverts our expectations of the bildungsroman but, as the *Newsweek* review of the book noted in 1982, introduces Celie "at about the point that most Greek tragedies reserve for the climax." From that point on, *The Color Purple* never strays from Celie's vantage point and forces us to stay present with her even as Pa's brutal violence against her body makes us want to look away.

Walker admitted as much two years after the novel arrived. "We are used to seeing rape from the rapist's point of view," she told the crowd at a National Writers Union conference on censorship and self-censorship held in New York City in the spring of 1984. "I could have written that Celie enjoyed her abuse and done it in such pretty, distancing language that many readers would have accepted it as normal." Walker eschewed the omniscient third-person narration more commonly used in Western novels, thereby making it unlikely that readers would feel sympathy for Pa by being immersed in his point of view. Instead, she instantly set up Celie's arc—of revelation and communal acceptance—at the very moment in which Pa renders her utterly defenseless. By speaking her truth, if at first only to herself, then to God, and finally to her sister, Celie begins her ultimate journey to self. To deny us access to Celie's viewpoint, Walker confessed, "would have been to betray Celie; not only her experience of rape, but the integrity of her life, her life itself."

And as much as Walker was focused on Celie's vantage point, she was also ruminating on the power of language. Since *The Third Life of Grange Copeland*, Walker had foregrounded violence against women as a main plot point. Until *The Color Purple*, however, she had never so boldly experimented with the twists and turns of vernacular speech. In that same lecture for the National Writers Union, Walker went on to tell her fellow writers that "it is language more than anything else that reveals and validates one's existence, and if that language we actually speak is denied us, then it is inevitable that the form we are permitted to assume historically will be one of caricatures, reflecting someone else's literary or social fantasy." To break that cycle, we know Walker did not shy away from Celie's reality but rather adorned her heroine with the speaking styles of Walker's own southern black family.

Before Alice gave birth to Celie, she had to kill a ghost.

Joel Chandler Harris still haunts Eatonton today. Born in 1848, almost a century before Walker, Harris became legendary for his "Uncle Remus" stories, humorous folktales collected during his encounters with enslaved African Americans on Joseph Turner's nearby Turnwold Plantation. Working as a journalist for Turner's pro-slavery newspaper the *Countryman*, Harris became intrigued by two enslaved African American men in particular, whom he knew as Uncle George Terrell and Old Harbert, and whose humor stayed with him for the rest of his career. He turned his plantation nostalgia into seven books, most notably *Uncle Remus: His Songs and His Sayings*, so he could "preserve in permanent shape those curious mementoes of a period that will no doubt be sadly misrepresented by historians of the future." Under Harris's purview, talented African American storytellers appeared as full-blown racist caricatures whose gibberish was hardly decipherable as English. Tragically, the stature of Uncle Remus stories only increased with each iteration, and it would take a century, a Civil War, and the civil rights movement for him to be put away. And even that was temporary.

Walker first fictionalized Remus's death in "Elethia," a semi-autobiographical short story published in 1981 in which the high school–aged title character steals and incinerates an Uncle Remus–like "Uncle Albert" dummy from a restaurant window only to discover later "Uncle Alberts all over the world" and "many Aunt Albertas" in her textbooks, in newspapers, and on television. Pulling on her own life, Walker, like Elethia, grew up surrounded by monuments and memorabilia of Harris's characters, Remus and Br'er Rabbit, all throughout Eatonton. As a young girl, she nurtured no animus toward Harris. She only knew his tales as told by her parents, Minnie and Willie Lee.

Walker reflected on this irony in "Uncle Remus, No Friend of Mine," a 2012 essay that appeared in a special issue of the *Georgia Review* on famed Georgia writers. Pulled from a talk that she delivered at the Atlanta Historical Society two decades earlier called "The Dummy in the Window," Walker painted an image of familiarity and intimacy. "Both of my parents were excellent storytellers, and wherever we lived, no matter how poor the house, we had fireplaces and a front porch." She continued, "It was around the fireplaces and on the porch that I first heard, from my parents' lips—my mother filling in my father's pauses and him filling in hers—the stories that I later learned were Uncle Remus stories." For Alice, Harris's folktales were the same as her family's black oral tradition.

So when her family ventured out to see Chandler's Uncle Remus in Disney's 1946 movie *Song of the South* at her town's segregated Pex Theatre, the idea that Uncle Remus was anything but admirable and welcoming had never entered her mind. But when the actor James Baskett appeared on the screen as Remus, she recalled experiencing "vast alienation, not only from the likes of Uncle Remus—in whom I saw aspects of my father, my mother, in fact all black people I knew who told these stories." She lamented,

"There I was, at an early age, separated from my own folk culture by an invention." Sitting in the balcony "colored section," Alice lowered her eyes as white families laughed at Remus's broken English as he told Br'er Rabbit and Br'er Fox trickster tales, and at his relationship with Johnny, a runaway seven-year-old white boy whom he coaxes back to his grandparents' slave plantation by singing "Zip-a-Dee-Doo-Dah." Wearing a floppy hat, full gray beard, and wide grin, the avuncular Remus disarmed Johnny as colorful, Disney-like animated birds fluttered on Remus's shoulders. For eight-year-old Alice, however, Remus suddenly surfaced as "a kinda talking teddy bear" that erected a "barrier between me and the stories that meant so much to me, the stories that could have meant so much to all of our children, the stories that they would have heard from us and not from Walt Disney."

When I walked around Eatonton in 2018, the town still celebrated Remus, though in moderation. Gone were the Uncle Remus Museum and the mannequin in the restaurant window. Harris's creations were sprinkled throughout town and, even more strangely, tethered to Walker's legacy. Right at the town's limits, before the Stuckey's gas station and mini-mart that sold MAGA hats and Confederate flag postcards, a sign welcomed tourists like me to historic Eatonton, "The Home of Joel Chandler Harris and Alice Walker." Inside the Georgia Writers Museum, a small storefront that stands fewer than two hundred feet away from the town's old Jim Crow movie theater, there are exhibitions dedicated to Harris, Walker, and Flannery O'Connor, rounding out local literati. One of the museum's great achievements was a large mural in the middle of town that displayed Celie and Nettie sharing a book in the background, an image of the trickster figure Br'er Rabbit sitting on a stack of Harris's books in the foreground.

By the time I entered Eatonton's biggest event venue, the Madison-Morgan Cultural Center, I felt that Walker's and Harris's fates had been so tightly bound here that no irony registered for me when I saw the gigantic poster of the movie *The Color Purple* hanging on a wall a few feet away from recently made watercolor paintings of Uncle Remus.

But this false equivalency was also just another betrayal. As I passed by a replica of the Pex Theatre's marquee and ticket window that triumphantly advertised *The Color Purple*, I conjured up Walker's own words: "Joel Chandler Harris and I lived in the same town, although nearly 100 years apart. As far as I'm concerned, he stole a good part of my heritage. How did he steal it? By making me ashamed of it." In due time, Celie became Walker's ultimate weapon in their duel.

Walker longed for a writer who appreciated and could express the vitality of black southern oral traditions, and she found it in Zora Neale Hurston and *Mules and Men*, her 1935 autobiographical collection of black southern folktales, a book that Walker took home to read to her family. "And it was the only thing they had ever heard in writing that they really got and laughed and understood," Walker tells me. "So, she was precious to me because I could see that we shared a culture." Recounting that moment in *In Search of Our Mothers' Gardens*, she wrote that "a kind of paradise was regained" as they sat around reading the book themselves and to each other. For "what Zora's book did was this: it gave them back all the stories they had forgotten or of which they'd grown ashamed that had been told to us years ago by our parents and grandparents." In Hurston, Walker found an ancestral writer whose ears were so sharp and whose pen was so powerful that they repaired years of cultural degradation. *Mules and Men* inspired Walker's mission to read all of Hurston's works, trace her biography, and then, in 1979, edit *I Love Myself When I Am Laughing . . . and Then Again When I Am Looking Mean and Impressive*, bringing together Hurston's folklore and reportage, her essays, and her fiction.

However, it was her experience with Hurston's *Their Eyes Were Watching God* that would change the course of Walker's career and enable her to have a notoriety unthinkable in Hurston's time. In graduate school, my professor Henry Louis Gates Jr. told us about the moment he realized that Alice Walker was "signifying" on Hurston, the term he used to describe a tradition in which black writers read and revised each other. Gates believed Hurston's novel was "the first example in our tradition of a speakerly text," a strategy that she used to emulate the sonic complexities of a black oral tradition. But, in addition to her characters' rich southern dialogue and their playing the dozens (a verbal duel based on comedic insults and sophisticated wordplay that began in slavery), he discovered an even more bold move that Hurston made midway in *Their Eyes*. The more empowered Janie became, the more her consciousness began to literally take over as the novel's narrator. "Dear Alice," Gates wrote as a young English professor at Yale University in the early 1980s while working on his book *The Signifying Monkey*, "I hoped only that you would see how much regard that I have for your work, and Zora's." He tepidly proceeded, "I wanted to show how your text revises *TEW* [*Their Eyes*], for *the critic*, whether or not you intended to." He went on, "With *TCP*, you have "placed" yourself in a line of descent from *ZNH* in a *formal* and textual way."

From Zora, Walker's inherited a model that taught her how to capture the complex speech patterns of rural black people as a novel's primary narrative voice. In *Their Eyes*, Hurston achieves this through what Gates identified as her use of "free indirect discourse," a literary technique that combines traditional third-person narration with some aspects of first-person speech. Halfway through the novel, as the widowed Janie finds sexual and social freedom through her romantic relationship with Tea Cake, a man around fifteen years her junior, the novel's third-person narrator begins to *sound* like Janie so much that it is unclear from whose perspective the novel is suddenly being told. One scene stands out: Janie, distraught by both her love of Tea Cake and her fear that he will leave her, is indistinguishable from the narrator:

> In the cool of the afternoon the fiend from hell specially sent to lovers arrived at Janie's ear. Doubt. All the fears that circumstance could provide and the heart feel, attacked her on every side. This was a new sensation for her, but no less excruciating. If only Tea Cake could make her certain!

I first met *Their Eyes* when I was a high school sophomore. Our English teacher, Alfonso Orsini, whose passion for reading dense prose was exuberant, cautioned us before we cracked the book open. We would have to be patient with Hurston's prose as we read to ourselves, alone, in our bedrooms. When he made us read out loud and to each other in class, however, I tightened up a bit. My white classmates had had so much fun mocking Jim's speech in *Huckleberry Finn* that I dreaded their newfound opportunity to blacken up—both their own speech and Hurston's characters'—and that a novel I had begun to privately fall in love with would become a full-blown coon show.

Hurston was castigated for taking such risks. While *Their Eyes Were Watching God* received a glowing review in the *New York Times*, Alain Locke, the famed father of the Harlem Renaissance, gave her a tepid review in the black journal *Opportunity*. "Her gift for poetic phrase, for rare dialect, and folk humor keep her flashing on the surface of her community and her characters and from diving down deep either to the inner psychology of characterization or to sharp analysis of the social background," he wrote. Locke believed Hurston's plot and prose were not combative enough to confront racism in their Jim Crow era.

Richard Wright, then a rising "race" writer from Mississippi, was even more excoriating of Hurston in his 1937 review for the Marxist magazine the *New Masses*. "Miss Hurston can write, but her prose is cloaked in that facile sensuality that has dogged Negro expression since the days of Phillis Wheatley," he blasted. "Miss Hurston voluntarily continues in her novel the tradition, which was forced upon the Negro in the theatre, that is, the minstrel technique that makes the 'white folks' laugh." Three years later, Wright's protest novel *Native Son*, about Bigger Thomas, a young black man fatally trapped by poverty, racism, and violence in Chicago, went on to become the first work by a black author chosen as a Book of the Month Club favorite, an honor that came with a lucrative increase in sales, while Hurston's work went out of print and she nearly starved.

Such history only sowed Walker's confusion and fear about her own literary fate. "If a woman who had given so much of obvious value to all of us, could be so casually pilloried and consigned to sneering oblivion," she wrote, "what chance would someone else—for example, myself—have?" But rather than push Hurston's prose away, Walker leaned in and contoured her epistolary narrative, a novel format that the British writer Samuel Richardson invented in 1740 in *Pamela; or, Virtue Rewarded*, to revel in the breadth and depth of southern black folk speech. As Mr. Orsini did with *Their Eyes*, every time I teach *The Color Purple*, I section off my class into small groups and ask my students to act out different scenes from the book so we can appreciate the candid humor and colorful language with which Celie narrates her world. Now I don't cringe when they recount the moment in which Celie first sees her daughter in a store with her adopted mother. "I seen my baby girl," she tells God. "I knowed it was her. She look just like me and my daddy. Like more us than us is ourself. She be tagging long hind a lady and they be dress just alike." In those few short sentences, Walker did something that only a couple of black writers before her dared to do: she fully transported us to the black South, enveloping us so much in Celie's worldview that with each page, we not only identified with her trauma but found ourselves willing her to leave Mr. _____, find her sister, and learn to love herself fully.

When Alice shared a draft of her manuscript with her editor, John Ferrone, and a small circle of friends, she was only partly prepared for the feedback they gave her. The black lesbian writer and poet Audre Lorde wrote to her, saying, "This is a beautiful book. It makes my soul-case jingle." Her gripe about Celie: "One thing—on p60 she speaks of Amazons & would she know what Amazons look like, or even the word? Nettie, yes, but Celie?" Picking up that thread on Nettie, her good friend John F. Callahan, an English professor at Lewis & Clark College, sent her a letter: "The question I want to raise is the form. Somehow, the 'Dear God' frame doesn't work for me. In fact, I prefer the letters from Nettie, that moralizing high rhetoric and all." He continued,

"I think Celie's a wonderful character, the voice you carry off so well just about all the time. All that's new, and I wish you'll come up with some new possibilities of form for her to speak her story." For these readers, Celie's informal speech suggests that she is not only more ignorant but also less believable than Nettie. Rather than pay heed to such advice, however, Alice refused to bend and to privilege Standard English, a language that she clearly associates with the colonizing mission of Christian missionaries in Africa or the racial authority of the typical third-person omniscient novel.

As an educated, churchgoing, well-traveled African American woman, Nettie and her formal writing serve an image of black womanhood that better resembles what we call "Race Women," historical figures like Mary Church Terrell and Mary McLeod Bethune, who espoused respectability politics as a way to defeat racism in the Jim Crow South. Alice does not radically alter Celie's sentence structure and verb tenses to mirror Nettie's, and therefore doesn't portray Celie's discovery of Nettie's letters as a pedagogical moment in which Nettie makes Celie more literate (as *The Color Purple* movie did). Nettie's letters serve to awaken Celie, help her fully realize the authority of her own voice, and empower her to leave Albert for good. By the end of *The Color Purple*, Walker completed the literary journey that Hurston could only partly do in her time by creating an entire literary universe around Celie and the voice.

Invoking Hurston's tone and topic during the end of the Black Arts movement, the artistic sister to the Black Power movement, was additionally risky for Walker. In Amiri Baraka's "Black Art," a 1966 poem long considered to have sparked the movement, he declared, ". . . we want 'poems that kill.' / Assassin poems, Poems that shoot / Guns." He went on to demand a black aesthetic whose sole purpose was to free black people from white supremacy. Hurston's folksy language and complicated romance plots had no place among those revolutionaries who claimed Richard Wright as their founding father.

"You know there's a page in my journals from the 1970s in which I'm talking about these four wonderful black men, male writers that I'm hanging out with in four different locations. And I managed to ask each of them something about Zora," Alice tells me as we sit on her couch and reminisce about Hurston. "And everyone says, 'I haven't read her.' Everyone. And these were wonderful writers. And I could've just sat right down on the floor and cried for them. Because how can you be so mean and so blasé, you know?" Walker's concern over Hurston's fate was a self-fulfilling prophecy.

In the summer of 1981, Walker sent an excerpt of *The Color Purple* to *Essence* because she assumed that publication, more than any other, would appreciate her liberation of Celie's voice and body. "Dear God," Celie says. "Shug Avery sit up in bed a little today. I wash and comb out her hair. She got the nottiest, shortest, kinkiest hair I ever saw, and I loves every strand of it."

Neither she nor her publishers were ready for the backlash waiting for her on the horizon. A hint of it, however, lay waiting in the mail.

"Dear Ms. Walker," the editor from *Essence* tersely wrote before declining Walker's submission. "Black people don't talk like that."

PART II

SHUG

4. OPENING THIS SECRET
TO THE WORLD

IN 1982, the night before Alice Walker was to pose for the cover of *Ms.* magazine, she sat in her bed fretting and coming up with a list of reasons why she should cancel. Lying next to her partner, Robert, Alice worried that her eye, which her brother Curtis blinded with his BB gun when she was eight, would tire and wander if she didn't get enough sleep. They, along with another brother Bobby, had been playing cowboys and Indians ("and because I was a girl, I did not get a gun. Instantly, I was relegated to the position of Indian," she later recalled), and rather than tell their parents of the incident, Bobby convinced Alice to lie and say she stepped on barbed wire. The pellet damaged her eye, and by the time she reached the doctor a week later, her eye, now scarred by an ugly cataract with whitish tissue, was about to worsen into a "sympathetic blindness" that would put her at risk for losing both eyes. The scar tissue on her eye, not rectified by an operation until she was fourteen, left her feeling so "disfigured and ugly" that her only relief was bookish solitude that took decades to overcome.

Thirty years after the incident, when Walker agreed to grace the cover of *Ms.*, her biggest fear was that her eye "won't be straight." But her real fears went deeper. "My meanest critics will say that I've sold out," she whispered to Robert. "My family will now realize that I write scandalous books." Despite having had such a long history of having her work published in and writing for the magazine, this was Alice's first time gracing the cover. In August 1972, *Ms.* editor Joanne Edgar first commissioned Alice's short story "Roselily." Walker and Gloria Steinem established their lifetime friendship shortly thereafter.

"I knew Alice before she met me," Steinem tells me as we sit in the living room of the same Upper East Side apartment where she has lived for more than forty years, a place that bears a striking resemblance to Steinem herself—eclectic and elegant, with a deep sense of personal history. Gone are the glasses; her hair, now a graying blonde, is pulled back in a ponytail; and her classic all-black shirt and pants are now updated with cowboy boots. "We had published her here early in the seventies before she came to New York. Once, when I was in Mississippi, I went to her house. But she and I have different memories of that gathering. I thought she was there, but she says she wasn't, just Mel Leventhal. Either way, I first fell in love with her as a writer."

By then, Steinem had established a reputation as a witty and probing writer. Her 1962 *Esquire* magazine article "The Moral Disarmament of Betty Coed" dealt with the contraception revolution that had begun sexually empowering young women on college campuses in the early sixties. The next year, she followed up with a groundbreaking story exposing the sexism and misogyny she experienced and witnessed while she worked undercover as a bunny for the Playboy Club. By 1968, Steinem's feminist politics and journalism were so intertwined that she decided to share her own experience of having an abortion overseas at age twenty-two in a piece about an abortion speak-out in a church basement for *New York* magazine. "There was something about seeing women tell the truth about their lives in public, and seeing women take seriously something that only happens to women," Steinem recalls during our conversation. "In my experience, things were only taken seriously if they also happened to men." Steinem took her magazine experience and, with the African American feminist activist Dorothy Pitman Hughes, launched *Ms.* magazine in 1972, the first periodical ever to be created, owned, and operated entirely by women. By then, Steinem, with her long blonde hair, aviator glasses, and subtle smile, emerged as the face of the women's liberation movement. Appearing again in *Esquire* that fall, Steinem's iconic look cut both ways. There, she was caustically dubbed "the intellectual's pinup."

Steinem was born ten years before Walker, to Ruth Nuneviller, a journalist, and Leo Steinem, an itinerant antique dealer, in Toledo, Ohio. Spending winters on the road with her father as he sold his wares from a house trailer, Steinem did not spend a full year in school until she was twelve. Steinem did not attend the Presbyterian church of her mother, or grow up in the Jewish synagogue of her father, but was a Theosophist, an adherent of a religion that she describes as a "very gentle and universal kind of belief." She credits her mother and her paternal grandmother for exposing her early on to this women-led and egalitarian practice, her first example of a prepatriarchal religion, one that drew her to Celie's expansive spirituality in *The Color Purple*.

"Alice's always ahead of me on the path," Steinem enthusiastically proclaims. "It's not a hierarchy, but I just feel like she's further ahead." Alongside sculptures from her early travels to India, Steinem's foyer is decorated with mementos from formative moments of her life: the cover of the first issue of *Ms.*; a photograph of Steinem and Susan Faludi, the author of the 1991 feminist manifesto *Backlash*, on the cover of *Time* magazine; and a letter from a cousin and his wife from 1969 disowning Steinem for tainting their good family name with her activism. Above them all is a poster-size piece of brown parchment paper bearing Walker's handwriting and the poem "She," given to her by Walker in 2009 on the occasion of Steinem's seventy-fifth birthday.

"I was so in love with her work that, once she moved to New York, I said, 'Why don't you come here as a part-time editor?' " Steinem reminisces. "So, she joined as a contributing editor, but Alice did not like meetings, which is the life of a magazine. So, people were sometimes put off by that, but I said, 'We can all work in different ways, she can just have an office of her own.' " Once on the masthead and earning an annual salary of $11,500, Walker distinguished herself by regularly publishing essays, reviews, and short stories, and also by publishing work by other black women writers. Despite such productivity, Walker eventually took a step back at *Ms.* after Celie and Shug demanded that she leave New York, and later San Francisco, for them to be born. By the time she moved to Boonville, Walker had quit her only job of three hundred dollars a month as a long-distance editor at *Ms.* because even that was too much of a distraction for her characters.

That Walker had never appeared on the cover of *Ms.* until *The Color Purple* was mainly circumstantial. "My house guest this weekend was Gloria Steinem who did a long interview for a cover story in *Ms.* to coincide with the publication of the book," Walker wrote in a letter to John Ferrone in November 1981. "They had wanted to do this for the stories but couldn't manage it." Walker went on, "She read the book on a plane ride from the Mormon Citadel in Salt Lake City where their God can be reached by computer. She loved [it], she says, and I believe her, and I think she will do everything she possibly can to help it out into the world."

Steinem was among the very few friends, including June Jordan and Audre Lorde, to whom Walker sent her early manuscript of *The Color Purple*. Steinem read the draft in one sitting in November 1981. In a letter to Alice that she excitedly scribbled midflight, she wrote, "I believe that you *are* a medium, but only a complicated magical medium and bring forth complicated magical people and you take people who seem full of hate and irredeemable (like Mr.) and then allow them to redeem themselves." Steinem then went on to praise the believability and accessibility of Celie's language and the "miracle" of Walker's ability to show humiliation, torture, and the truth without compromising the integrity of the story. Connecting the book to her recent trip to Utah, Steinem exasperatedly told Alice that the Mormon brides and grooms seal themselves to each other for eternity in sealing rooms with altars atop wall-to-wall carpeting and under crystal chandeliers. "Anyway, I would like to be sealed to you," Steinem mused. "Also, Celie and Nettie and Shug."

Steinem's stake in the novel's success extended far beyond that first reading. "At *Ms.*, we just decided this is a major American novelist and we did not care whether anyone else thought so or not," Steinem tells me. So she called the publicist at Harcourt and complained that the book's original print run of ten thousand copies was way too small. "Not to be pushy," she insisted. "But I told them, 'We're putting her on the cover as a major American author and I can't imagine anyone who reads this book is not going to agree.'"

In June 1982, Alice appeared with a short Afro on the cover of *Ms.*, betraying none of her dread from the night before the photo shoot. Gloria's article, slyly titled "Do You Know This Woman? She Knows You," was not merely the first major profile on Walker to date but a rare blend of friendliness, humor, and a prophetic flair. Steinem tells two stories: first, that African American women readers make up what Steinem calls a "small secret network" who already intimately and fully appreciate Alice's work. "Do you have *any* idea what she means to us?" she recalls a teary-eyed Spelman College student asking her. Then Steinem makes the case for Walker's influence on "white women and women of diverse ethnic backgrounds." But despite Walker's reach, her ubiquity and universality, Steinem also reminds *Ms.* readers that Walker's work still remains overlooked or underread. This move served two purposes: it celebrated Walker's unique literary style and acted as the first line of defense. "It is true that a disproportionate number of her hurtful, negative reviews have been by black men," Steinem's profile notes. "But those few seem to be reviewing their own conviction that black men should have everything white men have had, including dominance over women."

Such insights, while likely true, did little to ease those African Americans who long considered Walker's connection to Steinem as a cause for mistrust. "The idea that I divided the black community by supporting Alice was extremely painful and, of course, untrue," Steinem opines. But, at the time, even Marcia Gillespie, editor in chief of *Essence* from 1971 to 1980, concurred. Gillespie told Walker's biographer that, despite being a fan of Walker's writing, she kept her distance from her because Alice seemed so firmly connected to *Ms.* and Steinem. Gillespie, who later would become editor in chief at *Ms.*, said, "Back then, black women were extremely suspicious of women's liberation and the media's elevation of Gloria as the leader of the movement." Years later, Toni Morrison expressed even greater skepticism of Steinem's intentions: "I can't account for Gloria Steinem. She and Alice Walker are close friends." She went on, "What her agenda is, whether she represents white women in general, I really don't know." Saying that she personally was weary of such endorsements, Morrison told her interviewer that *Ms.* was right to be concerned about the early reception of the book. "It got bad reviews in the beginning and there was a consistent intention to dismiss the book on the part of publishing. It was only through such people [as Gloria Steinem] that it got attention," Morrison surmised. "Now somebody could say that their motives were suspect, you know. I don't know." For others, Walker's proximity to Steinem, coupled with Walker's previous interracial marriage to Leventhal, compromised her authority to speak on behalf of black people. "There was one guy who was very angry, campaigned against Alice by calling her my pawn." Steinem scoffed, "The idea that anyone could ever control Alice. It's so ridiculous, it's like controlling the ocean!"

That guy was Ishmael Reed, a literary satirist and author of *Mumbo Jumbo* (a novel that Harold Bloom listed as one of the five hundred most important novels in the Western canon). Reed was Walker's most relentless critic after the publication of *The Color Purple*. In a 1982 interview with the Australian newspaper the *National Leader*, Reed said, "There's the kamikaze feminist and the Gloria Steinem Axis, and the Black Feminist Auxiliary. I think Alice Walker is part of this group, which characterizes Black men as rapists." He went further: "Like a lot of frustrated movements, the feminist movement has turned to scapegoats and the Black man is it." What was at stake for Reed were the representations of the black male characters—Pa, Albert, and Harpo—whom he and, by the time the movie came out, several other black film critics and activists saw as racist stereotypes, characters there only to fulfill long-standing white myths of black men being innately sexually aggressive and violent.

In contrast, Steinem understood Albert and Harpo as Walker intended; they were figures of redemption, while their transformation was part of the pleasure and power of reading the book. But when I ask Steinem if she, Walker, and even Walker's publishers were a bit naïve in their marketing of *The Color Purple* given the tepid responses to Walker's earlier works, she says, "All along feminism was perceived as being anti-male no matter what. We were all man haters." A few seconds later, she admits, "I just was not prepared for this to be translated into Alice's work because it was fiction. I understood it better when it happened with Michele [Wallace], since that was journalism."

Appearing on the January 1979 cover of *Ms.* with her *Black Macho and the Myth of the Superwoman*, Michele Wallace, with her glorious Afro that extends beyond the page—overfilling the tight frame of the cover—glamorous makeup, and fiercely determined look, dawned a new era for the magazine as the first black woman on its cover, and for the feminist movement itself. A few months later the *Black Scholar*, the nation's third-oldest journal devoted to African American culture and politics, published a special issue called "Black Sexism Debate" in response to Wallace's book. In it, the sociologist Robert Staples's essay "A Response to Angry Black Feminists" diagnosed Wallace's critique of patriarchy as a result of her growing up middle-class, of being one of those who was "raised away from the realities of the black experience and tend to see it all as pathological in the same way whites view us."

Wallace totally rejected such stabs. "When it came time to promote the book," she recently said in an interview with *Vice*, "my publishers at Dial Press were adamant—despite the content of the book being feminist—that the book, that *I*, should not be described as feminist because it would doom the book financially. What could be worse than a feminist? A black feminist, it turns out."

It is even hard to remember now how divisive and negative those words were for people, distorting the reception of most black women writers who came of professional age in the 1970s and 1980s to such a degree that they were all automatically assumed to be black feminists. As Wallace was one of the first African American women to attract significant mainstream attention and to receive the full weight of those misogynist attacks, her experience was a harbinger for Walker's own fate. Even though Walker had yet to coin "womanism," a term she preferred over "feminism" because she found it more familiar and more southern, and thus truer for black folk, she couldn't avoid the anointing that happened once *The Color Purple* was in print.

Alice Walker was the face of black feminism.

Initially, the book reviews of *The Color Purple* were quite gracious. In his 1982 review "Some Letters Went to God," the *New York Times* staff writer Mel Watkins mainly praised it as a "striking and consummately well-written novel" in which "Alice Walker's choice and effective handling of the epistolary style has enabled her to tell a poignant tale of women's struggle for equality and independence." His main quibble with the novel was that it rejected the feedback Walker received on her manuscript drafts. Appreciating how Nettie's experiences as a missionary in West Africa expanded the novel's theme of female empowerment, Watkins often found Nettie's descriptions to be "mere monologues on African history." He continued, "Appearing, as they do, after Celie's intensely subjective voice has been established, they seem lackluster and intrusive."

Watkins's other concern, a feeling that seemed minor to him at the time, was "the somewhat pallid portraits of the males" throughout the book. Considering "the estrangement and violence that marked the relationships between Miss Walker's black men and women" the major theme of the book, Watkins complimented Walker's deft handling of the subject matter. By 1986, however, Watkins's tone had soured. In a lengthy essay for the *Times* on black women writers, he indicted Walker along with Morrison, Shange, Wallace, and Toni Cade Bambara for their increased portrayals of black men as oppressors and brutalizers of black women. In particular, he reflected on his review of *The Color Purple* and the reception of the novel: "For some, Miss Walker's skill as a writer was partially obscured by her one-dimensional portraits of black men. And, even at that time, there were murmurings and complaints about the alarming increase in stereotypical fictional portraits of black men as thieves, sadists, rapists and ne'er-do-wells."

Steinem saw homophobia in the resentment. "It was dirty laundry that threw some people: the abuse, lesbianism, the poverty. There was a belief among some black people that you shouldn't show these weaknesses to the outside world," she says with bemusement. "And then the success just magnified everything." It was Gloria herself who, while giving a lecture in San

Francisco in 1983, announced to Alice from the stage that *The Color Purple* had won the National Book Award for Hardcover Fiction. Though Alice had been shortlisted for the prize in poetry for her collection *Revolutionary Petunias* in 1973, Steinem was elated for Alice, as a friend of course, but even more so because Alice was a writer who had sacrificed so much in order to share her "secret with the world." That night, they went back to Alice's apartment to celebrate, and a few days later Alice received a call that changed her life: on April 18, 1983, Alice became the first black woman ever to win the Pulitzer Prize for Fiction.

The jury that year was chaired by the conservative writer Midge Decter (who was neither a novelist nor a critic) and had as additional judges John Clellon Holmes, the Beat novelist, and Peter Prescott, one of *The Color Purple*'s biggest supporters. In his radiant review of the novel for *Newsweek*, Prescott said it was "that rare sort of book" that was "an American novel of permanent importance."

Decter's first choice, Czeslaw Milosz's novel *The Issa Valley*, had originally been published in 1955 but was reprinted in paperback in 1982. Challenged by Prescott that this hardly reflected "excellence in the previous year" as outlined in the prize guidelines, Decter then named two other novels, claiming she couldn't come up with a third deserving choice. Decter only relented and agreed to bestow the prize upon Walker after Holmes and Prescott confronted her and threatened to expose her impropriety. In the award citation, Prescott pulled from his *Newsweek* review: "Love redeems, meanness kills—that is the novel's principal theme, as it has been the theme of most of the world's great fiction."

While Prescott extolled the book for its universality, others applauded it for its specificity, particularly the romance between

Celie and Shug Avery, a love that the *Washington Post* described in a profile of Walker as "physical as well as spiritual, a relationship that seems a bit unusual between two essentially rural southern black women in the 1940s." In that same story, before noting that "not surprisingly, Walker has a strong following among lesbians," the journalist Megan Rosenfeld asked Walker if she was worried about a negative response from readers about Shug and Celie's relationship. "There may be some people who are uncomfortable with the idea of women being lovers," Walker ventured. "But I feel they should outgrow that. Being able to love is more important than who you love." She contemplated, "If you love yourself as a woman, what's to prevent you from loving another woman? I think many women feel a sense of liberation about that part of the story."

The Color Purple wasn't the first African American novel with an explicit lesbian character. That status belonged to Ann Allen Shockley's 1974 *Loving Her*, a book that I first heard of when I was a sophomore in college in 1993. Shockley tells the story of Renay Davis, a working-class pianist who marries, has a daughter with, and is abused by Jerome, an African American whom she eventually leaves for Terry, a wealthy white woman writer. Though she and Terry ultimately end up together, it is only after Jerome beats Renay for her sexual transgressions and kidnaps and accidentally kills their daughter, which Renay believes to be her punishment from God for being lesbian. Mainly reviewed by feminist academics, *Loving Her*, when mentioned at all, mostly provoked animus in the black press. Claiming the novel was not black enough to be reviewed in the *Black World*, the critic Frank Lamont Phillips wrote, "This bullshit should not be tolerated."

Walker was one of the few writers of note to recognize

Loving Her's historical significance, even as far back as 1975. Couching her review in *Ms.* with the disclaimer that she didn't "know enough homosexuals of either sex" to be able to determine the accuracy of Shockley's characterization, Walker wrote that the novel "has immense value" because "it enables us to see and understand, perhaps for the first time, the choices certain women have made about how they will live their lives." Walker continued by saying it "allows us glimpses at physical intimacies between women that have been, in the past, deliberately ridiculed or obscured."

In African American women's literature class, our debates on *Loving Her* focused less on the presence of a lesbian relationship and more on Shockley's decision to make it an interracial love story. For my classmates who tended to mask their homophobia with Afrocentric racial pride, it was easy to say that Renay should not have been with a white woman. I remember a young black woman named Kafi who was two years my senior asking me, "What's worse for a black child? Growing up with two moms or one white mom?" Sadly, I didn't just shrug off the ridiculous nature of the question, my homophobia at odds with my feminist instincts. All I can say now is that when our class had to discuss Celie and Shug a few weeks later, we had to deal with the relationship between two black women on their own terms, with no interracial love to distract us.

For the black lesbian writer and activist Barbara Smith, *The Color Purple* was an extraordinary literary *and* political accomplishment. In her 1984 essay "Sexual Oppression Unmasked," Smith wrote, "What Walker has done for the time is to create an extended literary work whose subject is the sexual politics of Black life as experienced by ordinary Black people." Part review, part manifesto, Smith's piece challenged the growing chorus of detractors who publicly disapproved of Walker's book and its literary prominence. "Most gratifyingly, no Black novelist until Alice Walker in *The Color Purple* has so positively and fully depicted a Lesbian relationship between two black women, set in the familiar contexts of a traditional black community." She raved this was a "breakthrough in Black literature, because Walker so succinctly names the unnameable."

Other black women were offended by Shug and Celie. In 1984, Donna Green, an African American mother of an Oakland high school student, filed a formal complaint with the school district to protest what she considered the novel's inappropriate portrayal of folk language and religion and its excessive violence and "bias towards lesbianism." Fortunately, the six-member Oakland school board committee, which included the pioneering black feminist literary critic Barbara Christian, dismissed the complaint and unanimously agreed that the book had been used appropriately and affirmed that it should continue to be taught. Christian said that Ms. Green's rebuke of the language as denigrating was "extraordinary because it's probably the only book in America that uses black English in an aesthetically beautiful way." But even more significant was the impact *The Color Purple* had on young women who very much needed "the intellectual discussion" that the book stimulated.

For many, *The Color Purple* and Alice Walker were one and the same, leaving no sunlight between her literary imagination and her actual identity. The same year that the Oakland school district voted against banning the book, Walker received the biggest profile of her career. With one hand to the yellow notepad and the other on her forehead, Alice looked in midthought as she sat at her wooden desk in the photograph on the cover of the *New York Times Magazine*. The essay "Telling the Black Women's Story," by the author David Bradley, who was best known for his 1981 novel, *The Chaneysville Incident*, opens with the story of Walker's formative influence on Bradley's literary career. "I did not resolve to imitate her," he wrote. "I had enough sense to know that her way was not precisely mine—but I did decide to emulate her."

Seven years later, Bradley wrote that he "rediscovered Alice Walker through reading 'The Color Purple,'" an encounter that "almost did not happen" because "I had read enough about the book to want to avoid it like the plague." Calling the book "ground zero at a Hiroshima of controversy," Bradley at first attributed his reticence to Steinem's *Ms.* profile in which she had written about "an 'angry young novelist,'" male and implicitly black, who "had been miraculously tamed by Alice Walker's writing," and also to having "heard some people—not all of them white and/or male—expressing some misgivings about the book."

Bradley eventually admitted that the real origins of his distrust of the novel in particular, and of Walker in general, were more personal. "There is also much that dismays me," he wrote. "Other excesses are more troubling because they form, it seems, a pattern indicating that Alice Walker has a high level of enmity towards black men." He continued, "Yes indeed, I think, there is a world in Alice Walker's eye," referencing an essay that Walker wrote about Rebecca thinking her mother's eye was artificial. "It is etched there by pain and sacrifice, and it is probably too much to expect that anything so violently created would be free of some distortion."

Walker's friends ridiculed Bradley's essay. Mary Helen Washington, a literary critic and close acquaintance of Walker's, reassured her that the enmity belonged to Bradley, not Alice. "They put the wrong picture on the cover," she told Walker. "It should have been Bradley, since the piece was about him." Others complained directly to the *Times*. "Mr. Bradley trivializes the significance and literality of some of Miss Walker's male characters by psychoanalyzing her, a technique which even I, a psychiatrist, find as offensive in a magazine profile as at a party," wrote Miriam Rosenberg, a diplomate on the American Board of Psychiatry. "Perhaps the article itself illustrates one of the male tendencies which angers feminists: narcissism so blinding that it allows many men to incorporate and obliterate the achievements and identities of women." And even though Alice welcomed the sympathy and support, she had difficulty shrugging off Bradley's too easy dismissal of her earliest trauma. Publicly, she shared with the *Times*, "I regret David Bradley found me less likeable after discerning my feet of clay." She continued, "However, it may help him to know that my blind eye, also perceived by him as artificial, is in fact flesh and blood. Maybe my feet are, too." Privately her hurt was more palpable. "For such a well-done piece I hope he was paid 30 pieces in gold. I thought I was over any real pain regarding my eye, but apparently not," she wrote in her journal. "Just when I felt comfortable discussing its blindness, he writes in the *Times* that it is artificial" and "accounts for my 'distorted' vision, vis-a-vis black men."

That Sunday, however, another black man read that same *Times* feature and became even more intrigued with Alice. So much so that Quincy Jones, musician and producer of the world's best-selling album, *Thriller*, chose to bring only one book, *The Color Purple*, to read on his long-overdue vacation. Like Steinem, he read it in one sitting, later telling a reporter, "She really let God come straight through."

At the same time, back in Los Angeles, Peter Guber, the producer who had optioned the rights for *The Color Purple* for $65,000 right after it won the Pulitzer, was trying to track Jones down. Following Guber's massive success with the musically rich movie *Flashdance*, he wanted Jones to score this latest project. Jones took it as a sign. "It's been a secret dream of mine for years," Jones told a reporter about his decision to produce an African American art film.

Born on the South Side of Chicago in 1933, Jones was introduced to music by his mother, Sarah, who sang gospel hymns. When he was eight, Sarah was institutionalized as a result of a schizophrenic breakdown; his father, Quincy Sr., remarried and took his two sons to Seattle, where Quincy was exposed to jazz and blues clubs and first started playing the trumpet at fourteen years old. His maternal abandonment made him more sympathetic to Celie's tragedies. At the same time, Jones's itinerant upbringing allowed him to develop his love for music and movies during his adolescence. Recalling practicing with his bandmate Charles Taylor in his memoir, *Q*, Jones reflected, "We'd practice together for three, four hours a day in Charlie's house after school, then we'd go see a movie for eleven cents." He continued, "We'd play out our dreams in the movies too." After touring with jazz bands for several years, he moved to Hollywood to score films, landing his first one with Oscar winner Arne Sucksdorff's 1961 film *The Boy in the Tree*, and followed it in 1964 with Sidney Lumet's *The Pawnbroker*. In 1977, Jones won an Emmy for his soundtrack for the groundbreaking television miniseries *Roots*.

Jones, ever ambitious, wanted to make a predominantly black cast movie that could achieve critical acclaim. Sensing that Guber and his producing partner, Jon Peters, were overcommitted to other film projects, Jones pitched himself as the lead producer of *The Color Purple*. Jones then told Guber that Steven Spielberg was his first choice to direct. To which a skeptical Guber responded, "Maybe down the road." Convincing Spielberg, a filmmaker best known for the action blockbusters *Jaws* and *Raiders of the Lost Ark*, and the more sensitive hit *E.T.*, to direct a black-girl coming-of-age movie was Jones's first big challenge. But he believed Spielberg's name recognition, his expertise, and his empathy could imbue *The Color Purple* with the necessary gravitas and draw a diverse audience to this film. But before Jones could hire a director, or do anything, really, he would have to earn Alice Walker's blessing.

So, Jones began his courting. "I'll never forget today—you are so real, so beautiful—(even more so than I had imagined)," Jones wrote to Walker after their first meeting.

He signed off with a vow. "My promise still stands—(stronger than ever) we'll make a film that transcends anything before it."

5. READY TO WALTZ ON
DOWN TO HOLLYWOOD

ALICE WALKER SMILED as Quincy Jones's black stretch limo tried to turn into the small street leading to her modest San Francisco house. "(Well, Galilee Lane, of course it would be narrow!)," she wrote in her journal in the early morning of February 21, 1984. But when he stepped out, she thought he radiated. His coiled curls glistened, and he was, per usual, impeccably dressed. Steven, on the other hand, was disheveled and injured from breaking his two fingers by falling downstairs the night before his visit. A week before, Spielberg also broke his toes when he dropped his parrot cage on them. When Alice saw his plastered hand and toes, she instantly thought that he looked like "some kind of bird." But when he excitedly began to talk about The *Color Purple*, with such intelligence and sincerity, Alice was intrigued and Steven at ease.

A few minutes later, Walker amusedly joined Jones and Spielberg in their limo. More intrigued than anything else, she zealously listened as Steven recalled his own path to *The Color Purple*. His friend and fellow producer, Kathleen Kennedy, had casually given him the novel, telling him, "Here's something you might enjoy reading." Finding the series of letters an easy entry point into the novel, Spielberg finished reading within a few hours, only to find himself returning to it the next day, and then again the next month, before telling Kennedy that it really would make a great movie. Knowing that he was interested in exploring new kinds of movies, films that weren't necessarily expected of him, Kennedy suggested that Spielberg throw his director's hat in the ring. Years later, she'd recall, "I always believed he would feel confident at some point to do other things. That's why I brought him *The Color Purple*. After he read it, he said, 'I love this, because I'm scared to do it.'" Shortly thereafter, he reached out to Jones, who had signed on to the project only three months earlier.

Because *E.T.* had been his most serious film to date, Spielberg, as a thirty-seven-year old white, Jewish director, hesitated to pursue *The Color Purple*, unsure if he was the right person to bring Celie to the big screen. And yet, while he was producing *Gremlins*, the characters kept appearing to him. Of the book, he told the *Times*, "I came away from it very much in love with Celie. I was also obsessed with Mr." Spielberg connected to the novel on a visceral level because his parents divorced when he was fourteen, a traumatic experience that had a singular impact on his early storytelling.

"The whole thing about separation is something that runs very deep in anyone exposed to divorce," Spielberg said in an interview with the *New York Times*. "The breaking up of the mother and father is extremely traumatic from 4 up. All of us are still suffering the repercussions of a divorce that had to happen." Children being separated from their parents became a constant in his early films, like the parents searching for their baby in *The Sugarland Express*; a boy wrested from his mother in *Close Encounters of the Third Kind*; an alien separated from his home ship in *E.T. the Extra-Terrestrial*; a little girl abducted by ghosts in

Poltergeist. In *The Color Purple*, Spielberg saw parts of himself in Celie's abandonments by her mother, Pa, her children, and Nettie. In those chasms, Steven began to build out her world.

Once Jones discovered Spielberg *was* interested, he couldn't give up on the only director who he believed had the credentials to helm this project. Every time, Spielberg demurred, "Do you think a black director ought to do this film?" Jones countered, "Did you need to go to Mars to do *E.T.*?" And with that, Spielberg was hooked, and in spite of the fact that *Jaws* was the first film to earn $100 million, he agreed to direct *The Color Purple* movie for only $40,000, much of which he gave back to the film when they began to strain its $15 million budget.

Before meeting Spielberg, however, Walker pulled together a council of family and friends, who alongside Rebecca and Robert also included the literary critic and Berkeley professor Barbara Christian, the medical anthropologist Faith Mitchell, the writer and activist Daphne Muse, and the filmmaker Belvie Rooks. For most of the afternoon, everyone objected to the film. "Mainly because of what our experience has been with Hollywood and with white people trying to do black work," Walker wrote about their skepticism in *The Same River Twice*. For, like her, all the black people in her council bore the same racial scars that films like Disney's *Song of the South* had imprinted on her. "All you have to do is go to an average movie where you have one black person surrounded by a million white people, and you see how artificial the black character becomes. I did not want that."

But their faith in Quincy, Walker's own desire to reach a larger audience than her book did, and Jones's pledge that the movie would never embarrass black people persuaded Alice to at least hear Steven out, despite having never seen his most famous films, *Jaws* and *Raiders of the Lost Ark*, *and* missing Spielberg's most intimate film to date, *E.T.*, when it was in theaters. When Rebecca finally introduced *E.T.* to her mother, Alice, she saw parts of herself, lonely, empathetic, and misunderstood, in the figure of E.T. "Of all the characters being produced in Hollywood at the time, E.T. was the one that I felt closest to," Walker later remarked. "And if Steven could present this extraterrestrial being in a way that would make me feel more comfortable by having it have tea or working in the garden, then there was a possibility."

The prospect was made more likely as Alice, Quincy, and Steven discussed seeing Celie, Shug, and Nettie on the big screen over a four-course dinner at the landmark San Francisco restaurant Ernie's, getting tipsier and more excited about making the movie with every passing hour. With his strong grasp of the feeling and spirit of the book as well as his ability to convey her words visually, Spielberg soon convinced Walker. "Wouldn't it be great if you had Shug singing beautifully in one room," he imagined out loud to them. "And Squeak trying to mimic her in another room, right next door." In that moment, Alice began to see the story not as she had written it but rather through Spielberg's mind. Out of all her characters, it was Shug who was most ready to "waltz on down to Hollywood," and the more he spoke about his vision for the film, the more Walker trusted him to treat these women not as aliens to him but as kin.

Spielberg always knew that their dinner was in fact his final audition for Alice Walker. She'd later reflect on that meeting: "In ancient times, people believed that you thought with your heart." She continued, "They didn't really know about the brain. In more modern times, people say you think with your brain. There are a few of us who actually still think with our hearts, and after talking to Steven, I had a lot of confidence that he was one." After giving Steven her blessing to direct, Alice also seized the opportunity to make a different kind of movie history by changing the faces of those in front of as well as behind the camera.

In 1985, actors and producers were not using terms like "equity clauses" and "inclusion riders" to push for diversity in filmmaking. But in an attempt to prevent Warner Bros. from turning *The Color Purple* into *Gone with the Wind*, Walker sought additional assurances from Jones and Spielberg. In addition to agreeing to be a consultant on the project, Walker also demanded that at least half of the crew and those working off-screen be "women or blacks or Third World People." Keeping to his original pledge to protect her and her book, Jones agreed to let Alice have the last word on the fate of the film going forward, a decision made easier for Jones once Walker also agreed to work on the script with Spielberg.

Three hours later, after the limo dropped Walker off at home and took Quincy and Steven to the private Warner Bros. jet bound for Los Angeles, anxiety replaced Alice's giddiness. "I will write and confer. Write and confer," she wrote in her journal the next morning. "I feel some panic. I want so much for this to be good." She felt tired and torn, for not only had she promised Robert and her fourteen-year-old daughter, Rebecca, that she'd fully be theirs after writing the novel, winning the Pulitzer, and touring and interviewing for the book for the past year and a half, but she knew she had never written a script before and was worried about translating the novel's letters into a screenplay. "I hope you'll use me when you get ready to sketch the film," Spielberg wrote to her the next day. "I think I can make a contribution, but only when ready to receive." He ended, "Remember these words, Alice, 'NO

PRESSURE.'" And so, Alice relented, leaving behind her family and traveling back up to California wine country to make Celie, Shug, and Albert come alive again.

With the writing of the script in Alice's hands, Quincy and Steven began focusing on everything else: cast, crew, and scouting locations. Steven, after watching Danny Glover play the character Moze in the 1984 Oscar-winning film *Places in the Heart*, immediately approached him for the role of Mister/Albert and ended up casting him without an audition. Casting Celie ended up being a matter of luck and timing. Whoopi Goldberg had been performing in small comedy clubs in the Bay Area when Alice won the Pulitzer. She immediately read the book and a few weeks later found herself pulling over to the side of a San Francisco road just to listen to Alice reading from *The Color Purple* on NPR. Goldberg immediately wrote to Walker, saying that if ever a movie were to be made, she'd love to be considered for any part, even that of a "Venetian blind."

Months later, when Goldberg returned to her mother's house in New York, a purple envelope sat waiting for her. Inside, Walker's response: "Listen, I know your work, of course, and you are wonderful." What Goldberg did not know was that Jones had already asked Alice who she thought should play the part of Celie. To which Alice had easily suggested Whoopi Goldberg, a stand-up comedian whom Spielberg had never heard of. Because Spielberg had already been considering a lot of actresses to play Celie, and since she was unknown to him, Goldberg asked him if she could do her stand-up routine for him and a live audience.

That March, Goldberg brilliantly performed a ninety-minute routine before Walker, Jones, and Spielberg's curated crowd of Hollywood's A-listers. In the show she played characters, black and white, male and female, that included an elderly Jewish woman, a drug addict discovering Anne Frank, and a Valley girl opting for an abortion. "I knew you were Celie probably before you took your fifteenth breath," Spielberg later told her. "The reason I saw Celie in you in the first few minutes of your act was because of your strength. I would never hire a Celie who wasn't strong because you have to get there. That has to be in her DNA." Having never acted in a film before, Goldberg saw herself as a stage comedian and not a dramatic actress. On top of that, Goldberg saw little of herself in Celie, a reality that she used to her advantage. "The way I played Celie was to stand back from her," Whoopi told the film critic Roger Ebert when the movie came out. "Celie is so far away from me, it was easy to allow her pain to be there, because her life has so little to do with mine." Spielberg did his best to convince her she was right for the part by asking her to believe in his own process and expertise. "I think I'll know if you're that bad," he assured her.

Every once in a while, a new headline stated that Spielberg had cast another, more famous actress for the part, Spielberg even assuaging Goldberg's doubts that Diana Ross had landed the role. At the same time, Jones attended to Walker, who had instantly liked Goldberg's "sly gleam in her eye," a wit that Walker felt was essential for Celie's resilience and growth. When rumors swirled that Goldberg was going to South Africa to work on another project and wouldn't be able to do the film, Jones implored Walker to "put it out of your mind." He groaned, "It was only a rumor (we should have known)." But no letter from either Spielberg or Jones could calm Walker's own fears about writing the script. Unlike when she was writing the novel, few words rushed out of her and no characters tugged at her. And Walker had only ninety days to write their story.

"I've just typed out 65 pages of the screenplay and feel better than I have in two weeks," Alice wrote in her diary in March 1984. "And I feel good about this half (Now to worry about the second half!). We've reached the point of Celie leaving home. And perhaps the second half should open with her busy and happy in her Memphis life with Shug." Even with this breakthrough, Walker's depression was unmoved. "But I have the support of the Universe," she concluded, "and if I mediated more I would feel less alone." Alice was also aware that her loneliness cut both ways; the more time she dedicated to the script, the less time she had for Robert and especially Rebecca, whose increased physical ailments Walker believed to be symptomatic of her own maternal absence. Out of sorts, exhausted, and guilt-ridden for leaving her family again, Walker faced her biggest challenge: going back to a work that she'd already completed. "I just don't have the same kind of energy for it," she said. "But I did it again because I was beholden to the ancestors. I couldn't just say, 'You all go.' "

Responding to a casting question from Quincy about Shug's origins and sensibility, Alice playfully wrote, "I hardly know what to say about Shug Avery. It is like trying to explain a poem. If you could, you wouldn't have written the poem." Walker then goes on to describe Shug as a woman who is on a veritable search for freedom, a task made infinitely harder by a cold, critical mother, and by Albert, a passionate but sexually irresponsible and cowardly lover. The lifelong rejection of her by her own father, his church, Albert's father, and eventually Albert himself caused her to have several nervous breakdowns. Leaving her children and the South behind did not cure her pain; instead, her work as a domestic in the North and her indulgences and vulnerabilities pulled her back home and, over time, into the arms of Celie. "She is free of everything except the ability and need of love," she wrote to Jones.

Three months later, when Walker submitted the script, she hedged a bit by offering up two titles. "Some part of me was afraid that no matter how good his intentions, Steven's version of 'The Color Purple' would not deserve the name," Walker later wrote. "And so I created an alternative title for his film." Gone was the novel's epistolary framing. And now Shug is ever present. "SHUG took good care of me," Celie tells Albert near the end of Walker's script, an insight that relays Shug's pivotal role as Celie's lover and healer while also enabling Celie to begin her process of forgiving Albert as he seeks to redeem himself in her eyes.

Celie's confession is a small hint about how much screen time "Watch for Me in the Sunset" dedicates to Shug—for the story not only explores the Celie, Albert, and Shug triangle in Georgia but travels with Shug and Celie to Shug's Memphis home; on the road with Shug's blues band, as she takes on her much younger lover Germaine; and on their visit to reconnect with Shug's son, his wife, and their two children. By fleshing out her character and infusing Shug with emotional and sexual vulnerabilities that are more dormant in the novel, Walker's portrait of Shug serves to deepen our understanding of her bond with Celie. And it also makes Shug's later betrayal and fling with Germaine all the more heartbreaking, as Celie has not only dedicated her heart to Shug but upended her life to be with her. Even more impressive, Walker's script spent a great deal of time exploring Shug's house—its bedrooms, kitchen, and ultimately where she rehearses with her band, its "Upstairs"—in order to create a world in which Celie, Squeak, and Shug can be fully themselves.

And it is in this universe that we see and hear Shug as she likely imagined herself, as a blueswoman traveling nightclubs and juke joints, forthrightly and freely.

"I thought parts of it were extraordinary," Spielberg later admitted about Walker's script in an interview for the film's twentieth anniversary. "Because she not only adapted her novel, but she went beyond her own book to supplement it with other ideas. New, fresh ideas which is the whole process of screenwriting." Likewise, Lucy Fisher, senior vice president of the theatrical division at Warner Bros., applauded Walker's script. "I know it was painful, but you really did give us a good start," Fisher wrote. Despite such praise, Spielberg opted for another script. "I had completed one to my own satisfaction," Walker told her biographer. "It was, however, not the one Steven loved."

Spielberg went on to interview Hollywood's most famous screenwriters, with one of them telling him the book was ill-suited for film because its epistolary form was too difficult to adapt to the visual medium. But "the more I read *The Color Purple*," recalled Menno Meyjes, the Dutch writer who was up for Spielberg's sequel to *Raiders of the Lost Ark*, "the more I realized that it could *very easily* be made into a film." Understandably, Walker feared that, to an untrained ear, the subtlety of her rural dialect might connote dire poverty rather than more nuanced class dynamics—Albert owning land, Shug as a daughter of a preacher, and Celie as a shopkeeper—that made up black southern life. Whether or not the tall, skinny, and Dutch Meyjes would be able to pull it off, neither Spielberg nor Walker knew—but he had already read the novel twice on his own and identified whole chunks of the book that were visual. He saw his goal as taking those moments and entirely transforming them into a cinematic reality. More important to Walker, however, was Meyjes's proximity to the language itself. "He comes from a part of Holland that has its own folk speech which is looked down upon by people who speak standard Dutch," Walker reminisced to *Ms.* magazine in 1985. "And he had a real feeling for what folk speech is and how it's not substandard, just different." She noted, "I didn't have the feeling that Menno was a stranger." Greenlit by Spielberg and Walker, Meyjes retreated to a hotel room for three weeks, every morning sending ten to twelve draft pages to Spielberg, that had been looked over by Alice. Each day, while Steven was filming *Gremlins*, Menno waited on set to respond to Spielberg's red-inked feedback and they'd change it together that evening in what they called "Bible Class."

Once finished, Meyjes was too nervous to send his final draft to Walker. Waiting a few days before mailing it off, and then waiting a few more for her response, he was delighted that she approved. A now relieved Spielberg had one more request of her: Don't just be the talent behind the letters of *The Color Purple* but join him on set and work with him to make what Jones fondly called "our 'purple family'" come to life. At the same time, Spielberg, Jones, and the husband-and-wife production team of Kathleen Kennedy and Frank Marshall were still, after screening hundreds of actresses brought in by the African American casting director Reuben Cannon, looking for the rest of that family: Sofia and, even more distressing, Shug.

Believing that only a larger-than-life figure could embody Shug's sexual bawdiness and blues sensibility, Whoopi and Quincy favored Tina Turner for the role. ("If I'm going to kiss a woman, let it be Tina," Goldberg told Steinem at the time.) So, as he had done with Walker and Spielberg, Jones went on a broad campaign for her. In many ways, Turner, born Anna Mae Bullock in Nutbush, Tennessee, in 1939, who had just released *Private Dancer*, her fifth and by far most successful solo album, seemed ideal for the part. She could convey not only Shug's grit and charm with her voice but also—with her pink and blonde spiked hair, miniskirts, and denim bravado—an unusual amount of sexual autonomy. But Turner declined Jones, opting instead for the role of the ruthless leader Aunt Entity in the Mel Gibson–led movie *Mad Max Beyond Thunderdome*. "I lived Celie's life with Ike," she told Jones, referring to her fourteen-year abusive marriage to Ike Turner. "I don't want to live it again."

Sofia was easier to find. In early December 1985, Jones went to Chicago to testify in a copyright infringement suit against CBS Records regarding a song on Michael Jackson's hit album *Thriller*. Unable to sleep after his red-eye flight from L.A., Jones flipped through television stations until he landed on *A.M. Chicago*, a morning talk show hosted by a woman who had just arrived in Chicago from Baltimore that January. For thirty minutes, the buoyant, charismatic, thirty-one-year-old host named Oprah Winfrey captivated Jones's attention, after which he called Spielberg and changed the course of Winfrey's life forever.

Though Reuben Cannon initially resisted casting Oprah, he was even more unconvinced that Margaret Avery, an actress best known at the time for playing Belle Joplin in the biopic on Scott Joplin, was right for Shug. "I went out, got the book, read it, and connected so strongly with Shug Avery," she said, laughing, in an outtake interview about the film. "Aside from us sharing the same surname." Frantically searching for anything Shug-like, on the day before her audition, she found herself in a Hollywood

Boulevard porn shop buying a shimmery headdress made of red ostrich feathers. Cannon, much to his and her surprise, was so impressed that he forwarded her on to Spielberg the next day.

Sifting through the film's archives, marketing materials, interviews, documentaries, and even Walker's own book on the movie, I find little that explains the lack of enthusiasm about Avery's casting. Spielberg had forgotten that they had worked together on a television movie, *Something Evil*, in 1972. ("She had a very small part, she sang a jingle," he recalled.) After Turner, the dynamic singers Lola Falana and Patti LaBelle came up and Guber even suggested Diana Ross, who'd received a Best Actress Oscar nomination for playing Billie Holiday in *Lady Sings the Blues*. But in her synopsis about the characters in the film, Walker was quite clear that "Shug is modeled after one of my aunts who worked as a domestic in the North most of her life. I could never believe this because when she came to visit us—swathed in rhinestones (her diamonds) and furs (hand-me-downs from the woman she worked for)—you couldn't imagine her cleaning her own house, not to mention anybody else's." Stout, sexy, dark brown skin, and more akin to the actress Pearl Bailey, her aunt acted "like everyone imagines P. Bailey would act in an all-black-setting: assertive, funny, irreverent, unself-conscious, and relaxed." Walker also dampened any consideration of Diana Ross, who she thought would "make a much better Squeak."

Of all of those up for the part, Alice most loved Avery. In her journal, she noted, "Margaret, whom nobody seems to really like for the role, is wonderful, I think, as a Shug. And is, in many ways, the most vulnerable and brave of the actors, since she is aware that there are those who thought Tina Turner more appropriate." Years later in 2010, Avery, on *The Oprah Winfrey Show*'s twenty-fifth anniversary reunion celebration of *The Color Purple*, noted that making the movie, as a black woman in Hollywood, gave her such "a sense of self-worth" that she decided not to quit the profession and pursue acting for the rest of her life.

Spielberg's team had a substantially more difficult time finding a location that resembled Alice's actual southern community of Eatonton. Originally, Kokayi Ampah, an African American location manager later renowned for his settings in *The Shawshank Redemption* and *Million Dollar Baby*, wanted to film near Alice's childhood home, but the town had changed considerably since Walker left for Spelman, and even more so from the time of her grandparents. "An airplane flying overhead, for example, can ruin a scene that is supposed to take place in rural Georgia," Ampah said in a documentary about the film. Eventually, Ampah settled on the tiny village of Marshville, just outside of Monroe, North Carolina.

More secluded than the other spots in Georgia and Tennessee that Ampah looked at, Marshville stood out because he found a small house surrounded by lots of land that the production designer J. Michael Riva could use as Albert's house and then construct all the other elements—the church, Harpo and Sofia's home turned juke joint, and Celie's pants shop—around it. Likewise, they were able to transform a few blocks of the village itself into early twentieth-century blacksmith and tailor shops, post offices, and banks. They even flew in two planeloads of red Georgia clay to make the streets and sprayed the flowers in the fields a bright purple to ensure the set's faithfulness to the novel. The biggest difference: the racially segregated turn-of-the-century Marshville was now an interracial gathering, thanks to the cast and crew of *The Color Purple*—so much so that when the African American filmmaker

Elena Featherston, who had had unlimited access to Spielberg's set for her own documentary, *Visions of the Spirit: A Portrait of Alice Walker*, arrived at the Holiday Inn in Monroe to conduct her own interviews for her film, she immediately felt a familiarity. "It was as if I were back home in the Bay Area," she recalled after seeing so many of her friends laughing or playing cards together. The black and white cast and crew had not only taken over the hotel but somehow infused the entire town with the seamless interraciality that they carried with them wherever they went.

Alice, however, was suffering. "Dreamed I was at a large hall filled with enthusiastic, mostly white, people who were waiting for me to speak," Alice wrote in her journal on the first day of filming. "I was being introduced by a beaming white man who looked like the liberal version of Eatonton's (my tiny hometown in Georgia, pop. 4,800) mayor—sans crew cut. I was getting more and more nervous and couldn't decide what to read when he finished, as he piled on more and more platitudes." She ended, "I had no books. Nothing to read." Being on set triggered Alice's anxieties about selling the rights to her book *and* turning her story over to Meyjes and Spielberg. But her real fear was far greater: every day that she spent with the movie, away from either Eatonton or Boonville, Alice dreaded the fact that both she and her mother might be dying.

Shortly after Walker published *The Color Purple*, her mother had a major stroke, which left her paralyzed for the rest of her life. Before the stroke, Minnie Lou had read only the first few words of the novel. After the stroke, she was unable to sit upright in bed and read books. Over the years and up until her death in 1993, Walker's mother also suffered a series of ministrokes, each affliction more debilitating than the one before it. And as a result of knowing that her mother, who had barely been sick in Alice's childhood, was incapacitated, Alice too felt paralyzed. "It did not fall with a crash, but was rather a slow, inexorable collapse," Walker wrote about that period. "My legs seemed to be going out from under me. My heart felt waterlogged. My spirit lost its shine." Walker mourned, "My grief was kind enough to visit me only at night, in dreams: as I felt it wash over me, I did not care that I might drown."

Walker saw the movie as a journey back to the time in which her mother, her father, and her grandparents grew up. As Alice listened to the actors, she hoped that her mother would live long enough to see that world, her world, again. Watching Spielberg direct on the set, Alice amused herself with thoughts that he was making this gift for a woman whom he might never meet. More than any figure in her life, Alice's mother was also the person who nurtured her relationship with nature as a connection to God. When she wasn't cleaning the homes of Eatonton's white elite, Minnie Lou was in her garden, turning the land that sharecroppers toiled on into beautiful gardens. As Alice grieved her mother's confinement, almost three hundred miles away in Georgia, her own body began to turn against her in Monroe. She had new pains daily. First her eyes ached, and then her muscles and joints felt like they were splitting open. But she forged on, plagued by severe mood swings, sometimes unable to raise her arms or put one foot in front of the other. To help her move around the set members of the crew often carried her in her own director's chair or she walked with an elaborately carved dragon-headed cane that she had bought on a trip to Shanghai.

That pain, she'd later learn, was a symptom of Lyme disease. During the film shooting, it caused her to miss things on set that she'd normally catch, the subtle changes the movie made to her novel: the repeated scenes of Harpo, Albert's son and Sofia's husband, foolishly falling through the roof as he tried to build his house or repair the juke joint. ("Or maybe Steven assumed he was named with Harpo Marx in mind," Walker surmised. "He wasn't.") The most obvious revision was the fate of Albert, who stood apart from Celie's reunited family in the final shot of the movie. Walker, in her notes to Spielberg, insisted that Albert not sit on top of his horse because it further alienated him from the others, making him "too John Wayne–ish" rather than a man redeemed.

And then, of course, there was Shug. "In the part of the movie that was edited out of the finished version, there is a scene where Shug and Albert are about to make love against her best intelligence," Walker wrote in *The Same River Twice*. "And Celie, knowing this, and listening on the other side of the bedroom wall, begins to hum, 'Sister.' Shug hears her, 'remembers her name,' and leaves Albert high and dry." She goes on, "When I read my script, I see that in some ways it is also different than the book. What I have kept, which the film avoided entirely, is Shug's completely unapologetic self-acceptance as outlaw, renegade, rebel, and pagan; her zest in loving both women and men, younger and older." Shug shrank in the film, a result that Alice took personally because she was grappling with her own sexuality too. Her mother Minnie Lou's homophobic comments about Alice's cousin who was also her nurse struck a chord and she also felt betrayed by her partner, Robert, who told her that for over a year, he and his former girlfriend had been in a full-fledged affair. His reason: Alice was not sexually attentive and too distracted by her work.

"It was the timing of his confession that sent me reeling," Walker wrote. "Although his revelation came before there was public awareness about AIDS, I worried there might be a connection between his infidelity and my inexplicable illness." As she grew more ill, she felt even more vulnerable, and partly responsible for his infidelity. Admitting that their relationship was challenged by her need to live alone most of the time and her periods of creation and depression, she also believed that her bisexuality was a strain. "'I am an alcoholic, you are bisexual,' he'd joke with her. But Alice knew her adoration of and attraction to women was a source of concern for them both. "He often wondered if I loved him," she reflected. "And for how long."

A few weeks went by. She had another anxiety dream. Alice and a man duck into a crowded subway car to find safety from a riot. In the car are seated black and brown women and children. Walker blacks out and wakes up to find herself alone and wearing clothes that do not belong to her, her leather purse gone, her ID and credit cards missing. *I hadn't the faintest idea how to find my stuff*," she wrote. And in her reverie, people like Quincy Jones sympathetically listen but offer little help.

Quincy, of course, did not know about Alice's nightmare when he wrote a few weeks later with some bad news of his own. "I've been hoping this would go away, but evidently it won't," he said about a letter campaign mounting against their film. Launched that year by the Coalition Against Black Exploitation (CABE), a loose-knit group led by Earl Walter Jr. in Compton, California, its sole purpose was to safeguard black people from *The Color Purple*. Even before filming began, Walter asked for meetings with Warner Bros. and insisted that the film "uplift rather than degrade black people." More specifically, according to Walker's biographer, Evelyn White, they began calling for boycotts and distributing "action bulletins" against the film to national newspapers that read: "One must suspect a movie portrayal will focus on the dramatic visuals of homosexual play revealed in the book. One must also suspect this affectionate feminine display will be contrasted with an unfulfilling exchange between a black man and black woman." Shug and Celie's same-sex desire, coupled with Jones's music, "could be quite persuasive in pushing homosexuality as an attractive alternative to Black women's frustration with Black men." They asked, "What lyrics will Shug and others be singing? Will there be any positive male images in the movie?"

Though Jones and Spielberg insisted that these threats bore no impact on the movie itself, by the time Steven filmed Celie and Shug's most sexually passionate scene, he'd reduced it to a single kiss. "Anything more and the emphasis of the film would have shifted," Spielberg recalled years later. "There would have been just too much on that one taboo." Hearing out their concerns, Alice found their response—"to make it palatable," as Jones said to her—to be an artistic affront and personal betrayal. "I knew the passion of Celie's and Shug's relationship would be sacrificed when, on the day 'the kiss' was shot, Quincy reassured me that Steven had shot it 'five or six' different ways, all of them tasteful." She concluded, "The censor's knife scars the scene."

And yet, despite being in an overwhelming amount of physical pain, heartbroken, and deeply worried about her book's cinematic fate, Alice somehow still had faith in Quincy and in *his* Shug. "I will never forget the moment the phone rang, and Quincy Jones announced that they (he, Rod Temperton, and Lionel Ritchie) 'had it,'" Walker recalled in the liner notes for the film's soundtrack. "Meaning the theme song, the all-important song Shug sings to Celie in the juke joint. The song in which

Shug's love for Celie is first expressed." Jokingly realizing that "the brothers" came up with a tune better than she ever could have imagined, Walker stood in her kitchen, shaking her head, hands on her hips, and swayed to the luscious melody of Shug's song. "Damn," she said over and over again as the lyrics circled her.

On-screen, Avery's performance is even more seductive. Wearing a burnt-orange beaded flapper dress and a white and black feathered headdress, she shimmied her way to Goldberg. I show this scene to my undergrads when I am trying to explain the exuberance, iconicity, and self-possession of queer African American blueswomen like Ma Rainey and Bessie Smith in the 1920s. Having no access to video recordings of their stage performances, I find it hard, in our age of hypermedia, to convey adequately what made these women the most popular black performers onstage and on vinyl of the early twentieth century. But when I play the YouTube clip of Shug's bodacious performance, they always get it. "This song I'm about to sing is called 'Miss Celie's Blues,'" Shug announces, looking directly at a slightly embarrassed Celie, who is seated across from her. "Because she scratched out my head when I was ailing." Shug's coming out, followed by the horn player's sharp harmonic blast, is everything.

Sister, we're two of a kind
Sister, I'm keeping my eyes on you

Shug does in song what Spielberg was afraid to do in touch. In that two-minute sequence, Shug and Celie made history by being the first two black women to fall in love with each other on-screen.

6. LET THE FILM ROLL

I SAW SHUG give Celie her first kiss. Cupping Celie's chin ever so lightly, Shug stared at her newfound lover and warmly invited their lips to touch. Celie, in wonder, looked upward, and through Shug's eyes saw herself as worthy and desirable for the first time. Their caress, frozen in time, hung above me as I walked around the Art Gallery of Ontario in a room entirely dedicated to enormous images of their relationship as it unfolded in Spielberg's movie.

Together at *Femmes Noires*, the featured exhibition of Mickalene Thomas, an internationally celebrated African American visual artist, these images from *The Color Purple* took up an entire room at the Art Gallery of Ontario for four months beginning November 2018, and then again at the Contemporary Arts Center in New Orleans in a show that opened in November 2019. Inspired by watching the movie with her partner, Racquel Chevremont, in a hotel room in Brussels in 2015, Thomas started photographing stills of Spielberg's film. Over the next few months, through an elaborate procedure, Mickalene processed her negatives and turned them into images with translucent pinks, grays, and purples. Attaching reflective acrylic to her photographs, Thomas made her images wall-size, so we could see Celie and Shug as she did when she first saw them herself.

At thirteen, Mickalene asked her mother, Sandra Bush, to take her to see *The Color Purple* in New York City. Curious about the movie herself, Bush bought round-trip train tickets from Camden, New Jersey, in order to see the film. "My mother was very excited to see the movie," Mickalene told me. "But I also remember her being very surprised by how much abuse the actors reenacted. That was probably one of the first times for her to see that amongst black people depicted in film." She went on, "And I think that's why the movie resonated with her. I think she related to some of those women in it." Sandra's young marriage to her high school sweetheart was violent, with her teen husband even raping her at gunpoint before Mickalene and her brother were born. Divorcing him shortly thereafter, Sandra, at six-foot-one, pursued a career in fashion modeling while trying to raise her children by herself and, unconventionally, as both Buddhist and vegetarian in the 1980s. Her struggle for money was alleviated a bit when she took up with Eugene, a local drug dealer. Eventually, Eugene went to jail, Sandra became addicted to drugs, and Mickalene was estranged from her mother. When Mickalene asked Sandra to take her to see *The Color Purple*, she had long been living with her grandmother.

THOMAS SAW something else.

Now forty-eight, a graduate of two of our most elite art schools—Pratt and Yale—Thomas is best known for her monumental paintings of her "muses," black women like her mother, former lovers, her partner, Racquel, and occasionally celebrity icons like Michelle Obama and Oprah Winfrey. Thomas rose to art-world fame in 2012; her most iconic images show black women in recline, and partially nude, as a way of both honoring

Mickalene Thomas, *Shug Kisses Celie* (2016)
Silkscreen, ink, and acrylic on acrylic mirror mounted on wood panel
72 x 60 cm (28 3/8 x 23 5/8 inches).
©Mickalene Thomas, Courtesy of the artist

Mickalene Thomas, *Sister: Shug Avery Breakfast* (2016)
Silkscreen, ink, and acrylic on acrylic mirror mounted on wood panel
72 x 60 cm (28 3/8 x 23 5/8 inches).
©Mickalene Thomas, Courtesy of the artist

their sexuality and beauty and reversing the gaze of European painters like Manet and Matisse. While those white male artists similarly positioned black and North African women in their paintings, those figures were basically racial props, their bodies present, their power muted. Thomas's rhinestone-and-glitter-encrusted, jewel-toned, life-size collages sought to upset the narrative of those canonized images in the most audacious way possible: by returning the gaze to black women. Shug set Mickalene on her path.

"I was looking at the intimacy and the love between Shug and Celie," Thomas says. "At that point I was really starting to have really strong feelings towards other girls and question my own desires, but not know how to express that." At a private tour of the exhibition, Thomas—sporting cropped dreads and wearing a beaded tuxedo jacket, black pants, and sparkling sneaker boots—exuded a contained beauty and an intellectual confidence. As we walked around the exhibition, she told us about the four scenes she adapted from *The Color Purple*: Celie's love-struck look as Albert hurriedly prepares breakfast for Shug in the kitchen, Shug singing for Celie at Harpo's joint, Celie bashfully listening to Shug's performance, and the moment when they kiss in the bedroom, which showed me the limits of my own gaze. Her reflective aesthetic also reminded me of one of the few favorable reviews by a black male critic that greeted the film upon its arrival. "Watching this film is like returning to your own reflection in a mirror," Armond White wrote in the *City Sun* weekly newspaper. "You don't notice what others may see, you recognize traits distinctly familiar to yourself, perhaps marveling at their form and substance."

After leaving Mickalene's show, I became even more

intrigued by her ability to put herself in dialogue with *The Color Purple* by enabling Walker's characters to shine and us to see ourselves in them. I knew that I had always found solace in Celie, but until I began to understand the movie through Thomas's eyes, I realized I hadn't ever really seen Shug *and* Celie before.

And the truth is, I really hadn't. Homophobia always distorted my field of vision back in college. During my first semester on campus, as an avowed feminist, I could still be caught proudly wearing a "Silence = Death" T-shirt that I got at my first gay pride parade back in May of that year in Asbury Park, New Jersey. But to settle into my mostly black-friend world at Penn, I found myself undergoing a makeover. Swapping pink triangles for African head wraps, I attended Nation of Islam mosques, grew out my perm, and frequented Hakim's bookstore on Philadelphia's famed Fifty-Second Street. In those circles, homosexuality wasn't simply a disease but an existential threat that male-led black families had to root out in order to survive. A few months after being raped for the first time, I knew Celie's pain, but it would take another sexual assault and new secrets and feelings of shame for me to embrace the healing power of women's love and to tether my own fate to that of those pushed to the sexual margins of the black community.

Mickalene Thomas always knew better. Witnessing herself in Shug and Celie, she transformed Spielberg's chasteness into a real intimacy and simply gave us a new way to picture Walker's radical vision of love. Thomas tells me, "To sit there and see them on the large screen in surround sound helped me validate what I was feeling and not be confused by my emotions. I just remember sitting there completely transfixed, engaged, mesmerized, and just in it." She adds, "Not wanting the movie to ever end."

But in 1985, Alice Walker desperately wanted the movie to be over. Sitting in a private screening in early December, she cringed as she watched *The Color Purple* for the first time. "It looks slick, sanitized, and apolitical to me. Some of the words coming out of Shug and Celie's mouths are ludicrous. The film looks like a cartoon," she told herself. "I noticed only the flaws." She suffered a headache that stayed with her until the movie's official opening. "But it didn't turn out better because . . . ?" she asked herself. "All this week I've wanted to weep. I fear I have failed the ancestors."

The movie critics blamed Spielberg. "In Steven Spielberg's film version . . . the characters are also big and vibrant, but beyond that they resemble Miss Walker's barely at all," wrote the *New York Times* critic Janet Maslin. "Mr. Spielberg has looked on the sunny side of Miss Walker's novel, fashioning a grand, multi-hanky entertainment that is as pretty and lavish as the book is plain." The *Christian Science Monitor* was no kinder, proclaiming, "The fragmented phrases of the book, so expressive on the printed page, fight valiantly for life in Menno Meyjes's efficient screenplay." It scathed, "Spielberg's mass-appeal sensibility hunts them down and cleans them up, though, scrubbing and regimenting them within an inch of their lives. In place of the book's raw humanity, he gives us filmmaking by the numbers."

Some Hollywood insiders disliked Spielberg because they considered him an upstart, a filmmaker who, by taking on Walker's Pulitzer Prize–winning novel, had willed himself into the elite canon of arthouse filmmakers without paying the appropriate dues. For these detractors, the flurry of bad reviews was long overdue. "There are some great scenes and great performances in *The Color Purple*, but it is not a great film," the *Variety* review scolded. "Steven Spielberg's turn at 'serious' filmmaking is marred in more than one place by overblown production that threatens to drown in its own emotions." Likewise, Julie Salamon of the *Wall Street Journal* spared little: "From the moment this movie opens, with the pretty picture of young black women frolicking in a sunlit field of purple flowers, you get the sense that we are in for the *Sound of Music* approach of making it through hard times." She dug in: "Suffer a little, sing a little."

Rather than meet the reviews head-on, Spielberg, exhausted and "90 percent proud" of his movie, decided to take time off to be with his new baby, Max, and his wife, Amy Irving, who had gone into labor as her husband filmed Celie's own child-birth. Spielberg tried his best to ignore the complaints, taunts, and threats that the Coalition Against Black Exploitation made to boycott the film. Spielberg also paid little attention to movie critics and how it fared at the box office: A year after its release, *The Color Purple* was the first all-black-cast movie to gross over $100 million in American ticket sales.

The box office success did not stop the picket lines. After the film's opening in Washington, D.C., on December 20, Kwazi Geiggar, a member of the Coalition Against Black Exploitation, scheduled a boycott of the Los Angeles screening. "It portrays blacks in an extremely negative light," he told the *Los Angeles Times*. Four days later, Willis Edwards, the president of the Hollywood–Beverly Hills chapter of the NAACP, teamed up with Geiggar and carried protest signs that read "We Demand Artistic Responsibility," "Our Children Need Protection," "Are White Producers Trying to Destroy Black Men?," and "Who *Defines* Black Images?" Interviewed outside the theater, Edwards complained, "For the black male, the movie is very degrading."

Around the same time, Minister Louis Farrakhan, the leader of the Nation of Islam, hosted a special Chicago forum on *The Color Purple*. Donning his classic black suit, bow tie, and a twinkling smile, he attacked the movie before a mainly black female audience. "The movie starts with beauty but there is ugliness in the midst of this beauty," he said. Then, referencing his description of the film on the green chalkboard behind him, Farrakhan explained, "It starts off with the black man looking like a beast, acting like a beast, engendering the hatred of those in the audience for him." Of Albert's violence and Celie and Shug's turning to each other to heal, he proclaimed, "The bestiality of the black man leads to homosexuality." Ninety minutes later, in front of an adoring and applauding crowd, he demanded, "We must destroy *The Color Purple*."

These days when I talk about *The Color Purple* to my students, I have to not only tell them that the book was hotly debated but convince them *why* it was so controversial in the first place. And because the book and movie are so deeply woven into our memories of childhood and college years, even my peers don't remember the controversies. The story's enduring popularity is one reason for their amnesia. Another is that what made Walker's book so groundbreaking—Celie's sexual assault, Shug and Celie's same-sex desire, and Walker's own linking of sexism, racism, and classism without ranking them—are more mainstream than ever thanks to Marriage Equality as well as the black-women-founded Black Lives Matter and Me Too movements. In our current growing backlash against feminism, particularly by high-profile black men accused of sexual assault and harassment, like Russell Simmons and R. Kelly, the divisions among black people regarding *The Color Purple* feel strikingly uncannily and tragically familiar today.

The day after Farrakhan's speech, the *Times* ran the headline BLACKS IN HEATED DEBATE OVER THE COLOR PURPLE to report on over a thousand black people who had gathered at Chicago's Progressive Community Church in order to discuss the film. "No, it is not just a movie," said Nate Clay, the editor of the *Chicago Metro News*, a weekly black-owned newspaper. "It is a statement made out of context used as a pretext to take one more lick at society's rejects." Vernon Jarrett, a columnist for the *Chicago Sun-Times* and one of the film's most vociferous critics, contended, "Mr. Reagan, and his Attorney General, Mr. Meese, have decided that they are going to turn back the clock on us. The purpose of movies like this is to make it acceptable to you."

Black women, on the other hand, were more supportive. Maxine Waters, then a California state assemblywoman, helped to organize a special screening of the movie for the Black Women's Forum. She told the *Los Angeles Times*, "It was one of the most beautiful and most powerful films I have ever seen." She went on, "I was overwhelmed with the central theme of how one gains strength and comes into being. I don't find 'Color Purple' degrading or dehumanizing. That movie could have been about any color." Likewise, Congresswoman Shirley Chisholm, the first black woman to run for the American presidency, wrote to Alice directly about her novel: "It took me through the most intimate and most public trials, humiliations and joys in black women's lives. It dares to show us at our best and worst, to show us loving and changing and raising kids and fighting and dealing and winning and being friends." She concluded, "It makes our reality heroic—our regular, everyday selves." And everyday black women loved *The Color Purple* too. Eartis Thomas, a telephone company employee from Chicago, told the *New York Times* that she knew many Celies when she was growing up in Sunflower County, Mississippi. Because she, her mother, and her aunts were all victims of domestic violence, the movie "just lifted a burden." She insisted, "Black women should not be sacrificed for black men's pride. Let the film roll."

Danny Glover couldn't agree more. A few miles down the road, Glover, during the film's release, was co-starring in Athol Fugard's drama *A Lesson from Aloes* at Chicago's Steppenwolf Theatre. "Every community event in the city felt like it was about *The Color Purple*," he tells me. "People would come to my play and ask me about the movie. And I had to tell them spousal abuse and molestation is not something that just is in the white community, it is in ours too. So, I was in the thick of it when the movie came out."

At thirty-eight, Glover had found his breakthrough role in Albert. For his roles as a farmhand in *Places in the Heart*, a cowboy in *Silverado*, and a murderous Philly cop in the Oscar-nominated *Witness*, he'd already garnered lots of attention. "I had seen Danny in *Places in the Heart*, and I just thought he was remarkable. And I wanted to work with Danny very, very much, very badly," Spielberg said about Glover's casting in an interview at the time. "And I didn't have a second choice for Mister." Danny accepted the role for far more personal reasons. "I was the first person in my generation from my mother's side of the family to be born in San Francisco and not in the South," he told me during our interview. "But I spent the first few years of my life and every summer with my grandparents going to Georgia and working on the farm. My initial senses, the smells, tastes, sounds, the heaviness of heat, came from the South." In Celie, he saw his grandmother. "She was fourteen in 1909, the same age Celie would have been," he reflects. "And she's from rural Georgia, from a small town near Eatonton. So, I had my own ingrained memories from childhood that I brought to the role."

In February 2019, I saw *The Color Purple* in a movie theater for the first time. On a whim, I googled the movie name a few nights before and was pleasantly surprised that I was able to buy tickets for a one-night-only screening of the film at City Cinemas Village East. Too young to see it at the time of its release, I found that the big screen amplified Glover's quiet charisma, vulnerability, and youthfulness. Banking on Glover's likability going a long way toward helping audiences accept Mister's redemption, Warner Bros., in a story titled "Danny Glover: Villain in 'Color Purple' Is a Kind Family Man," marketed Glover's natural warmth by having him and his ten-year-old daughter, Mandisa, appear on the cover of *Jet* magazine in March 1986. "There is no comparison between the man called Mister in the movie and the one she calls 'Daddy,'" reads the article. The profile juxtaposed still shots from the movie by the famed photographer Gordon Parks with family portraits of Glover and his bright-eyed wife and daughter. Focusing on Glover as an idyllic and loving family man, the story eventually concluded, "In actuality, the character Mister could not be farther from the real-life Danny Glover. A tall, proud man, he is easy to talk to, warm, with a quick smile."

Walker felt something even more transformative in his performance, writing to Glover shortly after the film's release, "You have, in your acting, reached the level of healer." Describing her autocratic, drunk grandfather Henry Clay, she said, "Over the years I've struggled with this conflict: how to love someone who could destroy another human being." Midway through the film, Albert, dressed to the nines and carrying flowers, rushes out of his house to court Shug. Sensing a passion from him that she never knew in her actual grandfather, Walker welled up with "exquisitely happy tears." She knew Henry Clay loved her, but she simply couldn't forgive him for abusing her grandmother Rachel. But in Henry Clay's on-screen persona, Albert's adoration of Shug is undeniable. "It wasn't until I saw the movie that I fully realized how I had been longing and needing to be able to love my grandfather even as he was when he did the worst things," she acknowledged.

Even though Alice cared little if the film won an Oscar, she was bothered by the Academy of Motion Pictures' decision to ignore Glover's cinematic coup. With the movie's record-setting eleven Academy Award nominations, including for Best Picture, Best Actress for Goldberg, and Best Supporting Actress for both Avery and Winfrey, neither Glover nor Spielberg received a nod. The backlash against the film was so loud that on March 24, 1986, *The Color Purple* became the second movie ever to have the most Oscar nominations and not win a single one of them. That it lost to *Out of Africa*, the Sydney Pollack film starring Meryl Streep and Robert Redford, which was adapted from a novel by Isak Dinesen that basked in colonial fantasies of African primitivism and black inferiority, made their loss even more insulting.

"And that's the way it is," Quincy Jones told reporters about the film's loss at the Oscars afterparty at Spago restaurant that night. Someday we're going to have to change that." Goldberg, who lost the Best Actress award to Geraldine Page for *The Trip to*

Bountiful, was more biting. "I gave the Hollywood chapter of the NAACP the big old finger during the *Color Purple* thing," she told *Interview* magazine. "It cost us an Academy Award for that film. All the fervor that the NAACP created, saying the film misrepresented blacks." She blasted, "On one hand they scream that there's no work for blacks, and then when we get work we get our butts kicked for doing it."

In a public letter to a young African American woman named Mpinga whom she'd met at the University of California, Davis, right after the movie came out, and who had asked her about the movie, Alice wrote, "An early disappointment to me in some black men's response to my work—to *The Third Life of Grange Copeland* and *Meridian*, for instance—is their apparent inability to empathize with black women's suffering under sexism, their refusal even to acknowledge our struggles. A book and a movie that urged us to look at the oppression of women and children by men (and, to a lesser degree, by women) became the opportunity by which many black men drew attention to themselves."

The Oscar snub did little to quell the anger against the movie. In April 1986, Tony Brown, the host of one of the most respected independent black news TV shows, *Tony Brown's Journal*, opened "Purple Rage," his special episode on the movie, by saying, "You either love or you hate *The Color Purple*." Brown's four "experts" were all black men—no women—who divided themselves into two camps: whether the movie helped or harmed the black community. Two weeks later, as a guest on *The Phil Donahue Show*, Brown reiterated his disgust with the movie and even went so far as to claim that it was "the most racist depiction of black men since *The Birth of a Nation*."

Ishmael Reed's obsession with Walker's success was even more spiteful. Appearing on a talk show in 1986, he argued, "I think this movie is a political manifesto. She has said that men are evil in the *New York Times* magazine section, especially black men." He railed on, "She has said that lesbianism is wonderful."

"It was so lame, so ridiculous, and so untrue a lot of it," Walker tells me when I ask her about the backlash. "Some of it came with the book, but it was a lot worse with the movie, and then the criticism didn't stay on the movie. Someone tried to tie me to some agenda of bashing black men." But the controversy also took such a firm hold because it drew upon a stereotype that at the time was well-known among African Americans but far less familiar to white people: the black woman as race traitor. "Alice turned an unflinching and ultimately transformative and compassionate eye on the internal struggles within a black family," Walker's biographer, Evelyn White, tells me. "Also, Alice had married a Jewish white man, partly to break a law forbidding interracial marriage, so she was cast as an absolute traitor to the race by a large and vocal cohort of again, mainly black men and black women who bowed down to them and believed all the 'our black princes' bullshit from the 1960s." The controversy inspired White, who started working as a reporter at the *San Francisco Chronicle* in January 1986, to write Walker's biography. As she tells it, "I was amazed at the black folk who'd never attended a school board or city council meeting to protest inequalities among black communities in the San Francisco Bay area who all of a sudden found the time and energy to mobilize and protest the *Color Purple* movie. I was prompted to write my book about a decade later because I noted, over time, that Alice and her work seemed to drive such a diverse group of people nuts."

As a result of both the external backlash and her own internal struggles, Walker left the public eye, and retreated to Northern California to focus on her independent publishing company, Wild Trees Press. She also worked on her next novel, *The Temple of My Familiar*, an experience that she describes as "climbing into a whole other universe and closing the door behind me." Walker tells me, "It just lifted me above so much of the problem of criticism, and anger, and hostility. While people were tearing me to bits in town hall meetings and things, I was in this entirely other realm which was so splendid." Panned by some critics (but not, surprisingly by, Ishmael Reed), *The Temple of My Familiar* remains Walker's epic, a novel that traverses several periods, continents, and languages and is told from multiple vantage points. Decades before marriage equality became law, in the novel, Walker depicted Shug and Celie years past the ending of *The Color Purple* as two black women who live out their lives together as soul mates.

In *The Same River Twice*, Alice recalled trying to convince "my nephews, uncles, brothers, friends and former lovers that the monster they saw being projected was not the aunt, niece, sister, woman who loved them." Two years after Walker published those words, I had fully embraced being a black feminist after spending a few years post-college in therapy, individual and group, dealing with my own trauma from rape. I had broken up with my college boyfriend, whom I'd hurt more times than I care to admit, and was now in a new relationship with my future husband, Solomon, an African American man who had both a physical and emotional fortitude that required me to either rise to meet his unconditional love or bow out gracefully. I was on my way to a PhD program at Harvard to study African American literature, and, before going, I wanted to spend one last summer teaching in Philadelphia.

Walker later admitted that at the time she wrote *The Color Purple*, "the level of violence many people are living with today would have been unthinkable. Young black men, beautiful warriors without a cause and frequently without fathers, are killing themselves, each other, and other communities in a frenzy of despair." She lamented, "It is hard not to wonder what would have been the effect if young black men had been encouraged by other, older black men to listen to what black women writers, women and girls, have been saying and to understand it is not black men we want out of our lives, but violence."

The appeal of *The Color Purple*—Celie's extraordinary ability to invite me, Steven Spielberg, Quincy Jones, and my young African American male students into her world, not as mere spectators but as mirrors—speaks to the truth-telling power of the book. At twenty-one, I decided that I'd teach an African American film class for a group of teenage boys, mostly African American, who were mandated to attend this school as an alternative to prison. Of the eight movies we watched, only two captured their attention: *Belly*, a hip-hop–themed film featuring Nas that had come out the year before, and *The Color Purple*. To my surprise, not only had every student already seen Spielberg's film, but more than half of them knew all the words, miming Celie's curse, Shug's blues song, and Nettie's hand games without dropping a beat.

When I tried to bring up the controversy surrounding the book and movie, my students were bemused, with one young man confessing that he could see "some of that," but Celie's story was more powerful than "all that drama." And if my memory hasn't entirely betrayed me, I see him sitting there, baseball cap turned backward, slouched in his seat, wiping away a small tear that had built up in the corner of his eye when Celie and Nettie reunite at the end of the film, with Albert looking on, partly forgiven, the sunset behind him.

PART III

SOFIA

7. THE SINGLE MOST DEFINING EXPERIENCE I'VE EVER HAD

I REALLY WANTED to go to the Promised Land. Referencing Dr. Martin Luther King's 1968 "I've Been to the Mountaintop" speech, Oprah Winfrey's forty-two-acre luxury Montecito estate is right outside of Santa Barbara, California. Our interview was supposed to take place in the Tea House, a small, one-room building she constructed on her estate simply for the sake of cutting and storing flowers. As the Tea House began to take shape, Oprah realized that she wanted the space as her private sanctuary, a place on the property where she could go to read, meditate, and sit in her silence. "It's a commitment when I allow myself to come here," Oprah told *O, The Oprah Magazine*, a few years ago. "It's my dream, having a place like this. Some people ask, 'Why do you need more space?' And I tell them, 'I need it to restore myself.'"

That she never formally does business there—"no meetings, ever"—only increased my curiosity. Next to Alice Walker herself, there is no celebrity who has had her life impacted by or who has zealously supported *The Color Purple* more than Oprah Winfrey. And after making a pilgrimage to Alice at the top of her forty acres, I didn't want to miss seeing the place that the wealthiest and most influential black woman to ever live had made just for herself—and named after King's symbol of African American freedom—to be free. So my heart sank just a little when her publicist emailed me a few days before my trip to the Promised Land: "Would you be able to do it on Wed as well in LA if that was an option?"

So instead we would meet at the headquarters of the Oprah Winfrey Network (launched in 2011 under the acronym OWN), an eco-friendly five-story building in the middle of West Hollywood. The lobby is filled with plants, leather chairs, and videos of OWN's shows, like *Black Love*. As I waited for the older African American security guard to double-check my credentials, I peeked at my watch, silently frustrated at myself for sacrificing crucial minutes in my hotel room to prep for my in-person interview with Oprah. My heart started racing when I, wearing a red-, black-, and white-flowered kaftan dress, black ballet flats, and deep-red lipstick, got on the elevator, passing by the library with a complete set of Oprah's Book Club selections, and on the way up passed another floor with a huge, wooden *O* engraved into the wall done in the spirit of Mary Tyler Moore, Oprah's idol and the fictionalized feminist icon, whose apartment sported a giant *M*. I gave myself a pep talk as I walked onto her office floor, reminding myself that my only task was to ask a few questions to one of the most iconic interviewers ever to live.

Oprah admitted she was a ball of nerves when in 1985, at thirty-one years old, she walked into Steven Spielberg's Amblin Entertainment office to audition for the role of Sofia. Before she walked into his two-floor office building on the backlot of Universal Studios, Spielberg knew her only as the woman whom an insomniac Quincy Jones saw on morning television in a hotel in Chicago. Wearing a yellow shirt, a long black skirt, and a slight bobbed hairstyle, Winfrey had removed all evidence of morning talk show glamour and had stood before Spielberg as Sofia. Three decades later, as they walked arm in arm and toured Amblin again—this time on an episode of *Oprah's Next Chapter*—Steven asked her if she remembered how anxious she was when she auditioned for him there. She euphorically replied, "I remember everything because this is where I started the dream of my own studio."

That Oprah named her Chicago studio (where she recorded *The Oprah Winfrey Show* for twenty-five years) Harpo after herself (Oprah spelled backward) and her on-screen husband from *The Color Purple* in 1990 is only a small expression of her gratitude to Walker's novel. It is hard to find an interview with Winfrey in which she does not start her rags-to-riches tale with reading Mel Watkins's glowing review of *The Color Purple* in 1982. It was while in Baltimore, where she lived from 1978 to 1984, first working as a journalist and then as a co-host of the talk show *People Are Talking*, that Oprah came across the review. She says to me, "My life would have gone in a completely different direction without that experience. I was just sitting in bed with the *New York Times Book Review*. And that day I never got through the rest of the paper." Without a pause, she went on, "And as soon as I read that review, I got up, put my boots and a coat over my pajamas, and went to the bookstore and started reading and finishing the book that day before the bookstore closed."

Oprah immediately returned to the store to purchase all the remaining copies of *The Color Purple* in order to hand them out to every black woman she knew. "This was before Amazon. I said, 'Read this, read this, read this.' I'd just buy and hand out more and more books," she says. When she left Baltimore to host *A.M. Chicago* in January 1984, she still carried *The Color Purple* in her backpack. On her walks from the studio to her home, she gave out books to strangers, even at nail and hair salons, even to women under the hair dryers. Of her instant attraction to Celie's story, she says, "I opened the page and saw *Dear God, fourteen years old, what's happening to me? Being a girl who at fourteen years old who had a baby,* I was like, 'There's another human being with my story.'"

I knew Oprah's biography by heart. This was my third time interviewing her, with the previous two conversations taking place on the phone and for articles that I'd written on her for the *New York Times*. Anyone who watched daytime television in the 1990s or is familiar with *O* magazine, Oprah's Book Club, Weight Watchers, Dr. Phil, Rachael Ray, or the presidential candidate Barack Obama probably feels like she is his or her best friend. However, black girls of my generation, who watched Oprah from the comfort of our living rooms every day after school, she was more like our favorite aunt, the kind of woman we'd take advice from when our mothers were too strict or too uptight. For those unbaptized in the Gospel of Oprah, her story goes like this: a pair of teenagers named Vernita Lee and Vernon Winfrey in Kosciusko, one of the poorest and most segregated cities in Mississippi, gave birth to a girl in January 1954. Vernita's aunt Ida named the baby "Orpah," a Hebrew word for fawn, after a lesser-known woman from the book of Ruth in the Bible. But because everyone around her mispronounced the unusual name "Oprah," that somehow stuck.

Shortly after Vernita and Vernon broke up, Vernita left Oprah behind and moved to Milwaukee. Growing up with her grandmother, Oprah feared her grandfather. "One night my grandfather came into our room, and he was looming over the bed and my grandmother was saying to him, 'You gotta get back into bed now, come on, get back in bed,' " Winfrey told the *New York Times* in 1989. "I thought maybe he was going to kill both of us. I was 4. Scared." Oprah, believing her grandfather might strangle her at any moment, moved in with her mother.

It was different in the North, but no better. At nine, she was raped for the first time by a teenage cousin. Sensing a cold indifference from her mother, Oprah never told her. Over the next five years, Oprah was assaulted repeatedly by male relatives and friends who visited her home and had no real fear of being caught or punished. "When I went to tell my mother, her reaction was 'I don't want to hear it, just tell me it wasn't Willie [her boyfriend],' " Oprah says to me. Then she told her mother, "My instinct was right not to tell you, had I told you I would have been blamed." Out of desperation, Oprah ran away, only for Vernita to escort her daughter to a juvenile detention center. The only reason she was not admitted: all their beds were full.

Then in Nashville, Vernon and his new wife, Zelma, invited Oprah to live with them. She arrived, as she'd tell *Redbook* years later, ashamed and unconsciously blaming herself for "those men's acts." And she was also pregnant, a fact that she hid. Months later, she gave birth prematurely, and the baby died shortly thereafter. Oprah then told her father that she did not know her baby's paternity. One possibility, however, was his brother, who raped her when he picked her up from Milwaukee to bring her back south. "Everybody in the family sort of shoved it under the rock," Winfrey said in *Ebony*'s profile on her in 1993. "Once I told and nobody believed me, that was it. I wasn't the kind of kid who would persist in telling until somebody believes you." Teary-eyed, she pressed on, "I didn't think enough of myself to keep telling." Vernon and Oprah never talked about her pregnancy or baby ever again; it remained a family secret until her sister Patricia sold the story to the tabloids in 1990 for $19,000.

"I'll need tissues," Oprah warns me. A mix of casually tousled hair and camera-ready makeup, she leans over her desk with a framed photo of herself with Nelson Mandela and backdropped by several glistening Emmys. Tenderly pulling in her light blue suede jacket, Oprah adjusts her burgundy-rimmed glasses. "I always cry when I tell my *Color Purple* story. It was the single most defining experience I've ever had. It opened me up in ways I didn't even know." She presses on, "It showed me what love was, it showed me what it was to love your work. I loved being a part of this movie so much, I came to every scene whether I was in it or not. On my days off, I would come to the set just to watch other people."

Oprah never wanted anything so much in her life. Following Quincy's call to Steven after seeing her on TV in March of 1985, the casting director Reuben Cannon invited Oprah to screen test for "Moon Song," the code name that they used for the movie. To get to the audition on time, the flu-ridden Winfrey had to overcome subzero-degree Chicago weather and the police closing of ice-covered Michigan Avenue, so when she saw the script title, she couldn't help but ask Cannon, "Are you sure it's not *The Color Purple*? I have been praying for *The Color Purple*." But as soon as she began to utter the words from the script for "Moon Song" out loud, she knew they were Sofia's and left that meeting begging God for the opportunity to speak those lines on-screen.

Walker always imagined Sofia as a mélange, named after women whom she admired from afar or with whom she grew up. "Sofia. Sophia Loren and Miss Sophie, an independent woman I confused with Miss Lillie Orange who had a house on the hill, raised flowers and was husband and child free," Walker wrote in her key to the characters as she was drafting the novel. Drawn to these women's instincts for self-preservation and autonomy, Walker also based Sofia on Sophia, the goddess of wisdom, as well as on someone much closer: her mother, Minnie Lou, who like Sofia came from a family of twelve children, six boys and six girls. "All the girls had to be really strong because they had to outrun the white people," Alice tells me. "They'd encounter these horrible people sometimes coming home from church. White men who would try to rape them on horseback. And if the boys [their brothers] said anything, their fear was that they'd just be lynched. So, my mother, my aunts, had to run and just be really fast. And they were."

In both the novel and on-screen, Sofia Butler is a tour de force. Entering Celie's life about a quarter of the way into the book, we meet her at fifteen years old and as she courts Harpo in church, exuding confidence and assertiveness that up until that point we find only in the novel's male characters. In the film, we find her even more self-possessed when she arrives at Mister's house looking seven months pregnant and engaged to a love-struck Harpo. When Mister doubts Harpo's paternity, Sofia challenges his right to pose that question in the first place. After she and Harpo marry, they live together on Albert's property until Harpo grows frustrated by Sofia's independence and his own ineptitude. (In the movie, every time he tries to fix their broken roof, he falls through.) Following his father and Celie's advice to beat Sofia into submission, he slowly breaks up their marriage, to which Sofia responds by taking their children and retreating to her sister's house. By the time she returns, Harpo is in a new relationship with the much younger Mary Agnes (Squeak), and Sofia has taken on a new lover, a boxer named Buster Broadnax.

Sofia's larger-than-life presence offers Celie a defiant model of black womanhood that she had never seen before—and neither had we on the American screen.

After several months of not hearing from Reuben Cannon, Winfrey assumed she had lost the role because of her body size. "I'm fat, I'm overweight. This is finally catching up. Instead of losing weight, I gained weight," she told herself before checking into a weight loss center in Wisconsin to prepare for her first appearance on Johnny Carson's *Tonight Show*. She also dreaded losing a bet with the comedian Joan Rivers that she'd be able to keep the weight off. So, Oprah prayed and asked God to release her from her desires. She felt certain that Cannon did not want her after he chastised her for calling him two months after her audition to check in. Winfrey remembers him saying, "You don't call me, I'll call you. You know I have real actresses auditioning for this part. Alfre Woodard just stepped into my office. You have no experience. So, unless I call you, don't call me." Assuming that Spielberg had cast Alfre Woodard, an Emmy-winning and Oscar-nominated actress, for the part, Oprah says that in Wisconsin she began "to pray to bless Alfre Woodard in the role." Then, the instant she had made peace with losing the role, a staff member ran to her to tell her that she had a phone call. She recalled Cannon telling her from the other end of the phone line, "I hear you're at a fat farm. If you lose a pound you lose this part. Steven wants to see you in his office in California tomorrow."

Her producers on *A.M. Chicago* initially agreed to let Winfrey do *The Color Purple*; when they realized she'd be gone for several weeks they tried to pressure her to drop the film. Contracted to do 220 shows a year, she gave up her two weeks of vacation for the next couple of years. As a result of that tense horse trading, Oprah's lawyer William Becker suggested that the next time she was up to negotiate her contract, she should demand that the show be named after her. His reasoning: the next time a *Color Purple*–type project came along, Oprah should have no reason to refuse it. "I should never want to be in a position where I wanted to do something that badly and someone tells me I can't or I only have these many days off," she recalled him advising her. "So, I should own myself and take the risk and really bet on myself. That decision to own myself came about specifically because of *The Color Purple*." Within a few short years, her nationally syndicated *The Oprah Winfrey Show* became the highest-rated talk show in American history.

Being on set transformed Oprah in other ways too. Seeing Whoopi's mother gingerly attending to her daughter in between shoots, Oprah asked herself, *Is this what mothers and daughters do?*—a question that was triggered by her own feelings of maternal abandonment and abuse. She also experienced a solace and had spiritual epiphanies that she'd never known before. "I got to see what could happen when you work for something, give it your all, and then release it," Oprah tells me. "So, I live my life through give, offer, surrender." In between takes, she also watched as Alice, Steven, and Menno whispered notes to each other, altering the script ever so slightly, to make sure the scene reflected their mutual respect for each other and for their characters. "I learned to love people doing that film," Oprah told *Time* in 2001. For three days straight, as she sat on the grass outside of Albert's home and watched Spielberg shoot the same scene over and over again in front, she had an epiphany, writing in her journal, "This feels like passion, like love, when people come together with the common purpose."

On set, Alice shared pictures of Minnie Lou with Oprah.

"You remind me of her," Alice said as she sorted through a stack of images. Lingering on Minnie Lou's full-size silhouette, Oprah noticed that Minnie Lou was bigger, more robust than Willie Lee, a fact that made both Oprah and Willard Pugh, the actor playing Harpo, even more well suited for their roles than Oprah could have known. Sofia's defiance was even more extraordinary on-screen. Marching her way on the path to Mister's house with Harpo trailing her by a few feet, Sofia, pregnant, boisterous, and ever so in love with Harpo, commands the moment, entering the living room like a revelation, a woman who clearly can't conform to the sexist conventions or the racist expectations put on her in the Jim Crow South. "Sofia is a combination of so many women in my history," Oprah says to me. "I grew up with all these church-women around me. I used my aunt Ida. She was our matriarch."

Because Sofia rejects the oppressive categories into which she was born, her fall is devastating. After Harpo betrays her by trying to beat her into submission, she fights back and then takes her children and whatever love she has left for Harpo with her. But before she goes, she confronts Celie for advising Harpo to beat her in order to make her bend to his will. Stomping through the grassy field, Sofia gives one of the most memorable mono-logues of all time: "All my life I had to fight. I had to fight my daddy. I had to fight my uncles. I had to fight my brothers. A girl child ain't safe in a family of men, but I ain't never thought I'd have to fight in my own house!"

Oprah did that scene in one take. "That line was my anthem," Oprah recalls. "I didn't need anyone else there. I was saying that line for myself and every woman who has ever been sexually assaulted, molested, raped by an uncle, a cousin, a brother. 'A girl chile ain't safe in a world full of men.' I had to fight my brothers, my uncles, that's my story. I don't need anyone to help me tell that story." Oprah not only stole the scene, but over time, Sofia and Oprah became, in a way, indistinguishable from each other. In 1985, Oprah told a reporter that the tragedy of Sofia was that "she couldn't assert herself at that time in 1922" and "be who she wanted to be."

Oprah learned to exude Sofia's confidence off set as well. "Strong, independent, knows who she is," Oprah said of Sofia to the reporter Claire Olsen at the time of the film's release. "She was born before her time and she was proud of being a black woman, but she couldn't recognize that she couldn't do the same thing that white women do." Here, Oprah is referring to the scene in which Sofia, while traveling in town with her children, rebuffs attempts by the mayor's white wife, Millie, to pet her children and hire her as a maid. After becoming frustrated by Sofia's refusal of her offer, Millie enlists her husband to punish Sofia. Feeling cornered and under physical attack by the mayor, Sofia ends up punching him. That tragic scene ends with the sheriff, now accompanied by a group of white men, pistol-whipping and beating Sofia on the ground.

Sentenced to twelve years in prison for assaulting the mayor, Sofia is also partly blinded and paralyzed as a result of this mob attack. "No writer has made the intimate hurt of racism more palpable than Walker," Dinitia Smith wrote in her review of the novel in the *Nation* in 1982. Describing Sofia's early release from prison in order to serve the rest of her time working as a live-in domestic for Millie, Smith said, "In a fit of magnanimity, the Mayor's wife offers to drive Sofia home to see her children, whom she hasn't laid eyes on in years. The reunion lasts only fifteen minutes—then the Mayor's wife insists she drive her home." Oprah conveyed that aborted homecoming with such despair and broken dignity that she received an Oscar nomination for her first acting role ever.

Oprah says, "I knew I wasn't going to win. Gene Siskel told me, 'You're not going to win, so when you go to the luncheon, take the biscuit and bronze it.' It's now at the Smithsonian, my bronze biscuit." She believed then, as she does now, that the protests against the film damaged their chances to win. "Without a doubt the controversy is the reason we didn't take home a single award that night," she suggests. "I was puzzled and frustrated by the NAACP. There were so many black exploitation films and nobody said anything. And you choose Alice Walker? I think incest was part of it and admitting that is a thing that happens. And not wanting to have all black women labeled as that." She goes on, "By that time, I was doing a show, and I realized black men abuse their daughters and white men abuse their daughters. And I wondered why everyone thinks that story shouldn't be told."

Six months after losing the Oscar to Anjelica Huston for her role in her father John Huston's *Prizzi's Honor*, Oprah, with a layered bob and white-and-black-spotted shirt, looked directly into her talk show's camera and said, "I was raped by a relative. At the time, he was nineteen years old. I haven't seen or spoken to him since the day it happened. But I remember every single detail, you see." She went on, "There really is no darker secret than sexual abuse. I'm telling you about myself so maybe the closet where so many sexual abuse victims and so many molesters hide might swing open just a crack today and let some light in." She was right. Despite her producers' shock at her confession (she hadn't cleared her disclosure with them), a few and then a few hundred letters arrived at the station bearing similar stories. After that, Oprah went on to do over two hundred episodes on sexual abuse.

That day was a long time coming. "I remember when I was twenty-three or twenty-four and I told my lawyer at the time all my secrets. He told me not to tell anyone." A few months later, when a young African American woman went on Oprah's show in Baltimore and told her story, "that was the first time I realized I wasn't the only person. Her story was so much like mine," she recalls. "In the green room, I told her, 'That same thing happened to me; you're the only one that I heard with the same story.' She said, 'Why didn't you say something?'" Years later, Oprah answered her question as Celie would. A month before *The Color Purple* came out in theaters, Winfrey was interviewing a survivor of incest and childhood sexual abuse. After that, she said, "I got the courage to say, 'That happened to me too,' *live* on the air." For the next twenty-five years, *The Oprah Winfrey Show* told America its own story of childhood abuse and sexual assault. On any given afternoon, Oprah, on her comfortable beige couch and under warm studio lights, invited survivors of all ages and races into her studio, personalized her show to their experiences, and helped them break their own silence and end their lifelong shame. "I had no idea it was going to unleash the stuff that it did," she tells me. "My coming out about it caused a shift. I did not think it was going to start a movement. It was an honest reaction."

As she departed from the more investigative approaches to sexual assault that dominated the news media at the time or the more sociological style of *The Phil Donahue Show*, Oprah's show uniquely mixed spirituality, self-help, and a concerted effort to believe sexual assault survivors. Rather than reproduce the myth that most rapes are committed by strange men lurking in the bushes, Winfrey's show shredded that stereotype by having survivors, in episode after episode, tell us that more often than not their assailants were their cousins, friends, teachers, or, as in my case, young men they were dating. As a teenager, I simply assumed those weekday confessions were normal. I never knew a world before *The Oprah Winfrey Show*, so I grew up thinking that sexual assault was common, a far-too-prevalent rite of passage for children, particularly girls, in American society.

After my own rape during my first year of college, I knew of only a handful of African American women who had shared stories of sexual violence. Toni Morrison's *The Bluest Eye*, Maya Angelou's memoir *I Know Why the Caged Bird Sings*, Gloria Naylor's The *Women of Brewster Place*, Ntozake Shange's *For Colored Girls*, Walker's novel, and Oprah's show. Of them all, Oprah felt the closest to me because her show was unfiltered, on TV, and not in print. Seeing her so honestly struggle with her own body image, finding the right partner, and her own self-esteem muted some of the pain I felt and made me feel that the sadness and anger eating away at me was warranted and real. Twenty-six years after a young African American man in college raped me, I decided to participate in a ritual that I had witnessed so many times before. "I am a rape survivor too," I tell Oprah. That's all that I say. I don't tell her that the first time it happened, I was sixteen years old and dating a guy at the time who blared Bob Marley music to cover up my repeated cries of "*No!*" as he penetrated my body. As I twisted to get out from underneath him, he thrust harder, flipping me around, only to drive home his power by splitting me open from on top and behind. And I keep to myself that four years later and on my study abroad program in Kenya, I had another experience with rape in May 1995—that one even more brutal than the first, in a foreign country and by a near stranger who locked me in a room in Nairobi and pinned me down and forced himself on me. But I do give her insight into my almost-thirty-year recovery. I avert my eyes a bit and continue, "After I was raped in college, my sister began photographing my journey and, like Sofia, Shug, and Nettie, became crucial to my own healing. What helped you?"

"*The Color Purple* healed me," Oprah says. "Celie evolving and understanding her worth and her own beauty, her complete and total liberation by the end. It was so freeing for me and healing for me, a talisman, a spiritual comfort I carried around. And my show healed me," she adds. "That was my therapy."

Two years earlier, while interviewing Oprah about HBO's film adaptation of *The Immortal Life of Henrietta Lacks*, I told her I was struck by her character Diana's big revelation that she was a rape survivor, a fact that Rebecca Skloot's best-selling book mentioned only in passing. "One of the important themes of your work, from *The Color Purple* to *The Immortal Life*, is the sexual violence experienced by girls and young women. Why do you tell those stories?" I asked.

"I get to say, through the dramatic interpretation of these stories, what I tried to say [on *The Oprah Winfrey Show*] in stories of child molesters, victims of child abuse, talking to the molesters themselves, I tried and tried to make an impression on the consciousness of America about what sexual abuse looked like and its long-term effects. At the end of the show, it was the one thing I said I thought I failed at," she said by telephone. "That I couldn't get people to see it wasn't about the act, it was about the way we consciously accepted it. So, then I decided to dramatize it, and then maybe you can see it."

I bring up that conversation again when I finally interview her in person. This time we admit we are both quite emotionally raw from watching Dr. Christine Blasey Ford's testimony at Brett Kavanaugh's Supreme Court confirmation hearings in which Ford alleged that Kavanaugh had sexually assaulted her when they both were teenagers. Though much had changed since 1991 when we had watched Anita Hill come forward to accuse Clarence Thomas of sexual harassment, our moment of #MeToo meant that even though Ford might have been believed by the majority of Americans (Hill was not), that was still not enough to convince the Republican senators (and one Democrat) who confirmed his nomination in a 50–48 vote.

"The thing that has upset me the most of all the things that have happened in the last two years politically is the Mississippi rally with Trump mocking her," Oprah says. "You see the little boy behind her with this woman holding the 'Trump for Women' sign. I had a visceral reaction to that." She continues, "Where have we seen this before? I was thinking of her, Dr. Ford, and all the women who got the courage to say something. That's your fear: the soul's most offensive action is to be mocked and humiliated."

There is a scene—Sofia's second-most memorable one—in which she sits at the family Thanksgiving dinner table after she has been released from prison and the custody of the mayor's wife. Right after Celie stabs the table and accuses Albert of abuse and neglect and of his hiding Nettie's letters, a loud silence takes over the family dinner, during which Sofia, disfigured by the white mob's attack on her and with a head full of gray hair, at first groans and shakes her head in affirmation with Celie, and then lets out a full-body laugh. Each one of Sofia's utterances is an act of self-resurrection. "I've never told anybody this," Oprah says just before I get up to leave. "Just before I was going in to do that scene at the table, one of the makeup artists said, 'We need extra powder because fat black women sweat a lot.'" After a pause, she continues, "So I held that space of anger, disappointment, shame, and I sat there at the table rocking to the point where that became my mantra. I had only one line; that whole scene at the dinner table for me was an ad lib scene." As Oprah dabs her eye, tears flush mine. Apologizing for my breach of etiquette, I couldn't help but be overwhelmed. Celie attracted her to *The Color Purple*, but it was Sofia who pushed her to defy history. Two decades after Walker's first meeting with Oprah, Alice was even more exact: "I consider Oprah a contemporary goddess. For obvious reasons. But, I'll name a few," Alice typed in 2002. "Alice is Nurturing, Compassionate, and Loving. Fierce in her concern for All, and protective of those in need. Fierce also in defense of her Own beliefs, her own Sovereignty. She is incomprehensibly Powerful." Oprah appeared before me as an impossibility, and in many ways, she was. Alice had Zora. Oprah had Alice. I had all of them. Oprah had to break the mold in television to make her media empire, and if she weren't here, we wouldn't know how to invent her.

"Have you caught up with Sofia?" I ask.

"Not to the point where I punched somebody out. I have caught up with Sofia in the sense of not making a decision that is not going to benefit my whole self," Oprah tells me. "Just this week, I was asked about interviewing Ruth Bader Ginsburg, which I originally agreed to do. Then they came back with all these constraints, like 'You can't ask her about the court or current events.' Then I said, 'This week we can't talk about current events? You got the wrong person.' I can't do that. I literally said to her, 'I can't compromise myself to make things comfortable for everyone else.'" Noting how much she people pleased at the beginning of her career, Oprah reflects on her long journey to self: "When you don't feel you have the right to say no to someone actually touching your body, there's no boundary of your physical personhood. It takes a lifetime to learn to establish that."

8. I WAS STRUGGLING WITH FORGIVENESS AT THAT POINT IN MY LIFE

ON DECEMBER 1, 2005, the words "Oprah Winfrey Presents" flashed on the marquee right above *The Color Purple* at the Broadway Theatre in New York City. Now advertised in bold lights, the musical was a lifelong dream for the producer Scott Sanders, one he had been working on for almost a decade. Back in 1996, Sanders had pitched the idea to his boss, Peter Guber, the producer who had bought the movie rights to Walker's book after she won the Pulitzer in 1983. Sanders had stuck with the project, willing it into being, even personally financing its development for the first five years. By the time I met Sanders in July 2019, I'd planned no more than forty-five minutes of questions. I had never had contact with him before we met, and his staff, while courteous, were efficient, and quite clear that this conversation could only occur after I had been vetted, first by Alice and then by Oprah. Sanders was also in the middle of filming the movie version of Lin-Manuel Miranda's Tony Award–winning musical *In the Heights*, so I had to be squeezed in between his overnight film shoots and morning production meetings.

As I sat there in a casual navy maxi dress with white sneakers and matching summer jacket, I waved him over, assuming that he knew who I was because I was the only black woman in the restaurant. Sporting khaki shorts, a pin-striped open shirt, and smart sunglasses, he looked more Hamptons than Village, and after our warm embrace, he sat down and just jumped into the origin story of the musical *The Color Purple*. Two and a half hours (and countless iced teas) later, I realized that in the process of writing this book, I'd come across two kinds of people who are especially drawn to *The Color Purple*: the first, casual readers of the book or fans of the movie who affectionately remember their first encounter with Celie's story; and the second, like Quincy and Oprah, Scott and me, people who came across the book at such vulnerable points in their lives that the book became a talisman, with every subsequent return to it a way of marking time and healing wounds.

"During the filming of the movie, Quincy Jones called their team 'our purple people,'" I tell Scott. A bit more animated, I continue, "In writing this book, I discovered an intimate tribe, a few of the many millions of people whose lives have been changed because of reading *The Color Purple*." Knowingly smiling, Sanders agrees and admits that while he is still unsure why he had always envisioned Celie onstage, he always knew what the biggest obstacles would be: "First, I knew I had to meet Alice Walker. And then, I had to convince her to take *The Color Purple* to Broadway."

Sanders had an indirect route to theatrical production. By 1996, he had switched careers three times. First, he worked at Radio City Music Hall and promoted mainly African American musicians like Marvin Gaye, Kool & the Gang, and Diana Ross who, due to other concert promoters' racial bias, had difficulty securing gigs at other venues, like Madison Square Garden.

After fifteen years, Sanders left that job to work in television and film production for Peter Guber's media company, Mandalay Entertainment. Two years into his job as the newly appointed president of Mandalay Television, Sanders walked into Guber's office and asked if he could turn *The Color Purple* into a musical for Broadway. Intrigued by the idea of once again adapting the novel, Guber cautiously greenlit Sanders and even offered to introduce his protégé to his contacts at Warner Bros. "Honestly, I don't know where that question of mine came from," Sanders tells me.

It originated in his growing up in the South. Or at least the black South. As a teenager, Sanders was part of a small group of white students who helped integrate his hometown of St. Petersburg, Florida, by being bused across town to the predominantly African American Gibbs High School. "The white kids were ten percent or fifteen percent of the student population," Sanders says. "So, I had my first real exposure to black culture and black music when I was fifteen years old. I don't think I really understood how it was influencing me, but it was."

The year that Walker published *The Color Purple*, Sanders, just a few months into his twenty-third year, and a new graduate of the University of Florida, arrived in New York. Because of his rare crossing of the color line in reverse as an adolescent, Celie and Nettie were not strangers or stereotypes but characters quite similar to the real-life black girls with whom he came of age.

When Sanders read Walker's words in 1982, "I was struggling with forgiveness at that point in my life," he admits to me. "I couldn't understand Celie's ability to go through such hardship and challenges and continue to put one foot in front of the other every day and persevere. And while persevering, still be able to give love. And then most profoundly, her ability to forgive." He goes on, "That particular aspect of the story and her life really hit me hard. I understood hating Mister. And I remember saying to myself, 'Oh my God, I would love to be able to forgive like Celie does in *The Color Purple.*'"

Keeping his promise, Guber briefly introduced Sanders to Walker in early 1997, after which he immediately traveled to her brightly blue colored trilevel home in the Berkeley Hills in Berkeley, California. Standing in her lovely garden, with the Golden Gate Bridge off in a distance, Sanders was surprised to see Alice with a group of women friends whom she'd brought together to hear his pitch. "I told her how passionate I was," Sanders says. "And there's some elements to her story, in the book, that I feel could be looked at differently than the movie if we were able to put this on Broadway. I felt the Celie-Shug relationship definitely needed further exploration and enhancement. And knowing the way that some black men felt that she had vilified them in her writing, I thought that there was a lot more we could look at in her male characters, particularly the triad of Old Mister, Mister, and Harpo." Walker attentively listened as Sanders became more and more animated with each new plot point. Finally, when he finished, she kindly yet firmly responded, "Well, you seem like a very nice young man, but no."

Sanders pushed back ever so slightly. To which Walker replied, "You know, I've moved on. I'm writing other things. I've gone through this once. Turned the book into a movie and in many ways that was very painful for me. And I don't think I want to revisit that." But a year before, Walker had actually gone back to that period with *The Same River Twice*, in which she talked about the novel's jump from page to screen as well as the subsequent backlash as a series of "spiritual tests" that she needed to overcome before moving forward. "You really cannot step into the same river twice," Walker wrote, believing that by publicly sharing her experience with the movie, she would release herself from *The Color Purple* and all its controversies, once and for all.

Still, Sanders had a small dash of hope. "She could have said to Peter, 'No, I'm not interested,'" Sanders says of Guber's initial introduction to her. "So, I reached out to her again and very uncharacteristically of me I asked her: 'Why don't you just let me fly you to New York for a week and let's just go see some shows. And let's talk.'" Once she arrived in New York, he immediately wanted to show her how much musical theater had evolved since she had seen *Jesus Christ Superstar* in 1977. So, in August 1997, he took her and her good friend Gloria Steinem out to see two musicals: *The Fantasticks* and Savion Glover's *Bring in 'Da Noise, Bring in 'Da Funk*, a musical retelling of African American history from slavery to the present through the complex polyrhythms of tap dance. The show was up for nine Tony nominations that year; Glover ended up being the third African American to win for best choreography, while George C. Wolfe remains one of only two black directors to receive the award for best direction. In turn, Sanders assumed that Walker and Steinem would be so impressed by its historical sweep as well as its artistic innovation that they would begin to see how it was possible for Celie's words to liven up the stage too.

Sanders's other problem was persuading Alice that he, as a white, gay man from the Gulf Coast of Florida, was the right person to produce *The Color Purple* on Broadway. So, the next night, he rented a dinner cruise ship, invited a cross section of artists, producers, and friends, including Diana Ross and James L. Nederlander, the founder of the nation's largest family-owned theater company, and circled New York Harbor in honor of Walker. "This is your reference cruise. I'm going to go sit in the back and you feel free to ask anybody on this boat whatever you want about me," he said to her. "To just see if they think I am worthy of you giving me this coveted piece of material of yours, your child if you will."

Before the trip, Alice had called Sanders's friends Whoopi Goldberg and Bette Midler. During the harbor ride, she talked to Diana Ross, whose favorable opinion of Sanders underscored what Goldberg and Midler had impressed upon Walker. "'If anybody can do it, Scott Sanders can,'" Walker remembers them saying. Since their initial meeting, she had come to admire Sanders's diligence and deep humanity. "I knew that even if we did something together and it failed, it would be perfectly fine," Walker later recalled in the official souvenir book from the *Color Purple* musical. "We would have learned wonderful things about life, and it would have been a very good journey."

Scott knew he had to assemble as diverse a writing team as possible despite the increasing skepticism he met from theater industry gatekeepers who thought the book's themes of incest and domestic violence were too bleak for Broadway. So, Sanders improvised by asking prominent Tony Award–winning composers as well as jazz, R & B, and pop musicians to write songs and submit them like an audition tape. Sometimes, Sanders would ask his friend, the Tony Award–winning composer Susan Birkenhead, to write him lyrics that he could then take to songwriters like Stevie Wonder, Terence Blanchard, and BeBe Winans. "I felt like *The Color Purple* had to have its own unique sound," he says. Two years later, he was still looking.

Through his Grammy Award–winning friend Allee Willis, famous for her own collaborations with Earth, Wind & Fire, Sanders met the Grammy-nominated African American singer and songwriter Brenda Russell, who along with the drummer and songwriter Stephen Bray pitched the idea of all of them writing songs together. Choosing a scene that had a variety of mood changes and multiple characters coming and going, to demonstrate their ability to orchestrate and interpret the musical changes in the story, they sent Sanders two songs (one of which, "Shug Avery Comin' to Town," made it to Broadway). "I remember getting these songs from Brenda, Allee, and Stephen. And I called Alice, put the CD on, held my cell phone up to the stereo, and said, 'I think we found it.' And she said, 'I think we did too,'" he continues.

Sanders then asked Marsha Norman, who won the Pulitzer Prize for Drama the same year as Walker for her play *'night, Mother*, to write the musical's book. "The *Color Purple* musical's authors were three women, Allee, Brenda, and Marsha. Two African Americans, Brenda and Stephen. And then there was me, a white, gay man who had never produced a musical before in my life," Sanders reflects. "This was the team. And I remember there were people, there were Broadway purists at the time, that said to me, 'What are you doing? These people have never written a musical before. You've never produced a musical before.' And blindly, naïvely, passionately, we just did it. We just kept going."

And going. Over the next few years, Sanders self-funded the early stages of the production, which generated a two-and-a-half-hour libretto that picked up the pieces that Walker felt Spielberg had avoided: a more expansive exploration of Celie and Shug's intimacy and Albert's arc of redemption. Following Celie's abuse, sexual and spiritual awakening, and forgiveness of Albert and love for Shug, the story, told in two acts and punctuated by big songs like "Any Little Thing" and "What About Love?," deliberately stays pretty close to the plot of Alice Walker's novel.

During our meeting, I'm embarrassed to tell Scott that I never saw the original Broadway production. Though I was intrigued by the concept at the time, I also could never fully wrap my head around the idea of a musical. I was unsure how Celie's story and Walker's radical politics could appear in the more upbeat genre and tourist-driven industry of Broadway. I flirted with the idea of taking my mother-in-law, then sixty years old, a black woman raised in North Carolina, and my mother, then fifty years old, a musician from Newark, because I thought they, not I, were the ideal demographic for the show. So, before my conversation with him, I spent hours at the New York Public Library for the Performing Arts at Lincoln Center, watching several iterations of the musical: from its Atlanta tryouts to its 2005 Broadway run, its revival in 2011, and its national tour today. Sitting in front of a small computer monitor with headphones, I tried to take the most copious notes possible. In order for me to watch these recordings, per the library's request, I had to agree that I'd only watch the performance on the premises, a once-in-a-lifetime viewing. In all those versions, I was startled the most by Sofia's evolution. Dressed in a cream blouse and purple pants, at the end of the 2016 performance, Sofia stands beside Celie, forming a new triangle of sisterhood with her and Shug. Nettie, around whom the novel revolves, recedes to the background. This is partly because the script is so disciplined in its focus on Celie

("She's the spine and the engine of the story," Sanders says) that Nettie's life as a missionary in Africa is abbreviated so as not to distract the live audience with too many competing characters and plot turns.

But it is also because Sofia is the heroine best suited for our moment. "We did some focus groups with all black women who said 'I love this book, I love this movie, but if I'm going to Broadway, I want to have a good time and I'm concerned that this is just going to make me sad,'" Sanders shares. "So, we really had to listen to that, and think about [it] . . . I mean, I remember talking to the authors and saying, 'How fast can you get Sofia on that stage?'" Recalling those early days of writing, Sanders goes on, "Because she's the first ray of light, hope, and sunshine on that stage. And I asked the authors, I remember, 'Can you make it happen in ten minutes?' As it turned out, it was about twenty."

Likewise, Gary Griffin, the director of the original Broadway production, describes her character as paramount: "The show's life depends on Sofia. We take you to some dark areas, and the hope that Sofia will return is a nice thing to have." Griffin continues, "We see Sofia triumph. And we see her at rock bottom." As a result, next to Celie, Sofia has the most sobering arc in the entire story. By unapologetically embracing her black womanhood, she defies her own time and increasingly belongs in ours. So much so that, by curtain close, she is the woman who we, in the audience, like Celie, most want to be.

Unlike in the movie, however, onstage Sofia is not blind, limp, and wearing a wig full of gray hair to mark her own deterioration after being brutally beaten by a white mob. She is still a victim of their white rage—in the musical she is arrested and forced into domestic servitude—but her violence is told *to us* rather than being performed out in the open. Because the musical has no white actors, I've often wondered if that is why so many white people in the audience feel comfortable with this version of *The Color Purple*, their absence reading as an absolution. Sanders rids me of this notion: "We had the mayor's wife and mayor in our pre-Broadway show in Atlanta, Georgia, in 2004. Two reasons informed their removal. One, we didn't feel we absolutely needed them to tell the story." He goes on, "Perhaps the most practical and creative reason was if you have the mayor and his wife as characters in your show, you need understudies for both and now you have four members of your cast for a scene that is less than ten minutes long. And we're sitting there in Atlanta doing a postmortem of the whole show and we said, 'If we got rid of the mayor and his wife, we could have four more African American dancers in the show.'"

One of the more subtle results of Sofia becoming more iconic in the musical was that Harpo's character became more multidimensional and his arc more transformative. "I felt that Harpo in the movie was more of a comic foil than he was a fully fleshed-out character," Sanders says to me. "And yet, it kept resonating with me that this son makes some huge departures from his father and his grandfather. First and foremost, he chooses the most feminist, independent woman in town to be his bride. Even though he professes to Celie that he wants someone that he can tell what to do, just like Pa tells her what to do. In truth, he was attracted to Sofia and you don't get attracted to Sofia if you want someone to just obey you. So, there was a contradiction there and I thought Harpo is the next generation—or, if you will, the first generation—in that family to break away from those norms and traditions. And wouldn't it be interesting to look at him further."

As the writers did workshops of the show in Atlanta, they realized that they needed a song just for Harpo and Sofia. "We need it to be really sexy," recalled Marsha Norman. "They start out fussing and end up sexed up and ready to go." They cast Felicia P. Fields, who earned a Tony nod for her role as Sofia, and Brandon Victor Dixon, who was nominated for his role as Harpo—and who is now famed for *Hamilton* and for winning a Tony for the 2014 revival of *Hedwig and the Angry Inch*. The chemistry between the two actors was striking and their duet—a sultry, lively, youthful song called "Any Little Thing"—was flirtatious and upbeat. Though the characters are supposed to be hard at work, the song climaxes with a heavily panting Sofia jumping onto Harpo's hips. Occurring after Sofia has already been beaten by the sheriff, incarcerated, and forced into domestic servitude, this moment is especially cathartic for the couple onstage and for the audience, as Harpo uses his love for her to bring her back to life.

Sitting next to Sanders, Alice quietly watched Dixon's Harpo and Fields's Sofia resurrect her parents' passion for each other when the musical previewed at the Alliance Theatre in Atlanta, Georgia, in 2004. Walker, a mere hour from her hometown, didn't know what to feel exactly. "Scott lost weight sitting next to me in Atlanta," she told an interviewer. "I knew that I would have to tell the truth, and I was so sorry that he was sitting there. And the first feeling of anything is so difficult, because it's really hard to see the completed thing separate from all that has gone before." She went on, "This happened with the film, too. So that was very hard. I liked it, but I wasn't wholehearted." She left the theater that evening without saying a word.

The next night, she returned and thought it was utterly

fabulous. "It took the second evening seeing the show—just as it had taken the second viewing of the film—to really see it," Walker said at the time. "It had only to do with my own need to let all previous things fall away so I could see what they were actually offering." In fact, she left loving it so much that she was suddenly afraid that Broadway might ruin it. But it didn't. Sanders was still in previews in Atlanta when he learned that the Broadway Theatre was now suddenly available after *The Mambo Kings* pulled out due to production delays. They would have to speed up their own schedule.

Sanders, now with Quincy Jones, Oprah Winfrey, Bob and Harvey Weinstein, and the private equity funder Roy Furman on board as producers, hoped black audiences would embrace their *Color Purple* as earnestly and generously as they had in Atlanta. Eleven million dollars were invested in the show, but it turned out to be a shrewd investment. During the show's run from December 1, 2005, through February 24, 2008, it cultivated an extremely diverse Broadway audience. In a special *Today* episode on *The Color Purple*, the show reported that, unlike the nearby *Wicked*, the Broadway Theatre hosted "a mix of blacks and whites, kids in hoodies and older folks in suits and ties, kente cloth alongside leather jackets."

The theater critics weren't as impressed, a reality that Sanders reminds me of by quoting Ben Brantley's 2005 *New York Times* review. Brantley not only opined that the show was unable to "fan sparks into a steady flame" but that the music was written by a trio of songwriters who "clearly have a knack for clingy, synthetically tasty melodies adorned with spicy regional accents (rather like Cajun-style Kentucky Fried Chicken)." As with the movie, these lackluster reviews did little to deter audiences. Groups made up mainly of black women, from churches and club organizations, from all over the country, traveled to see Celie triumph. So much so that within five months of its opening, *The Color Purple* was grossing more than $1 million a week. At the same time, Broadway experienced a significant demographic shift. In 2006, in large part due to the fifty-fifty black and white audience split of *The Color Purple*, the number of nonwhite Broadway theatergoers had increased by 17 percent—reaching the highest proportion in recorded history.

The show entered the 2006 Tony Awards with eleven nominations, the most after the musical comedy *The Drowsy Chaperone*. But it won only one award, LaChanze taking home Best Actress honors for her role as Celie. It lost Best Musical and Best Lighting to *Jersey Boys*, and Best Book, Best Score, Best Scenic Design, and Best Costume Design to *The Drowsy Chaperone*. Best Choreography went to *The Pajama Game*. Nevertheless, the show was profitable, and it went on to tour nationally from 2007 until 2012.

I knew that this original run of *The Color Purple* was not widely regarded as an artistic triumph, so when I asked Sanders why he thought it had revived so well, first with its premiere in London in August 2013 and then again on Broadway in 2015, I wasn't sure if he would answer candidly. Although London investors had expressed interest in bringing over the Broadway version years before, Sanders later admitted in an interview with the *New York Times* that he was worried that the show's content and its "highly emotional American sensibility" would be unappealing to British theatergoers. Concerned that the show had yet to reach an international market, Sanders reached out to David Babani, the artistic director of the Chocolate Factory, a theater renowned for scaling down works. Babani confessed to missing the musical on Broadway ("I was a bit snobbish in my thinking—'It's not aimed at me, it's another adaptation of a movie,'" he said in an interview with the *New York Times*). But after Scott encouraged him to see a non-Equity production in 2010 in Riverside, California, Babani committed resources to the show, even recruiting the Scottish director John Doyle, a Tony Award winner acclaimed for transferring Stephen Sondheim and Hugh Wheeler's *Sweeney Todd* from London to Broadway with virtually no set.

At first, Doyle scoffed at the idea. Of his conversation with Babani, Doyle says to me, "I told him he was mad for a number of reasons. I mean, it was just like an instinctual reaction. I had seen the original. It was big, right? It was literal." He continues, "If he wanted a re-creation of it in any way, then I wasn't his guy. Plus, I'm white, I'm male, those are two good reasons for me not to do *The Color Purple*. I'm British, the director should be an American." Sitting in his office chair in mid-Manhattan, Doyle's words betray something else: a singsong accent that sounds more Caribbean than mainland British. When I tell him that, he responds, "That makes sense. I'm from the Highlands of Scotland. It's the same tune." But his familiarity with black life, particularly with southern black folk, was far more formative. Earning a theater scholarship at the University of Georgia in Athens in the 1970s, Doyle spoke to a black person for the first time in his life on the Greyhound ride down from New York to Atlanta. Though the campus remained fairly socially segregated, as a twentysomething student, Doyle nurtured his attachment to and affinity for the South. "I knew Putnam County," he tells me. "I knew where the story happens, right?" He goes on, "I come from a very religious background, in a different kind of religion—I mean, it's still

Christian religion, but a different way of that worship. But I knew, by being in Georgia, I knew what a gospel church was. I knew what a Baptist church was. I understood what it was. Which I think in another circumstance I probably wouldn't." Of his college years in Georgia, Doyle concludes, "It made me, that's the thing. All of that experience of life-changing experiences, inevitably they affect you and the artist that you become."

The world of *The Color Purple* that Doyle ended up creating was based on his firsthand experience living near Walker's hometown. He describes his signature aesthetic as "essentialism," a style that he refined in small, often financially struggling theaters where actors had to embrace a minimalist stage to convey a more complex story line. By the time that he took on Celie's story, he had earned a reputation for making shows that are in many ways anti-Broadway, partly because of his thoughtful chiseling away of bombast and excess. Doyle not only designed the set with ochre-colored floorboards based on his memory of African-American homes and "their porches that have a hint of Georgia clay," but he also stripped away the more extravagant and varied set of the original, leaving wooden porch chairs to serve as the main backdrop and props for the show. "I wanted the back wall to say something about brokenness," Doyle says. "Remember the slats and the brokenness in the slats? I wanted to say that this is about poverty. It's about people who don't have a lot. Which is why there weren't many props or anything. They don't have much."

I've seen Doyle's version three times. Twice live, and the third time on tape. The live version did not have Cynthia Erivo, whom Doyle himself cast for both the London and New York runs. She was born to play Celie onstage. In his 2015 review, Ben

Brantley revised his earlier *Times* review: "That earlier 'Color Purple,' a box-office hit, was a big, gaudy, lumbering creature that felt oversold and overdressed. The current version is a slim, fleet-footed beauty, simply attired and beguilingly modest. Don't be deceived, though, by its air of humility." He concluded, "There's a deep wealth of power within its restraint." In turn, in *New York* magazine, the theater critic Jesse Green called it "one of the greatest revivals ever" and wrote that "Doyle's intervention amounts to a kind of theatrical CPR, restarting the heart of a show that, in its original production, seemed to die before your eyes." That next year at the Tonys, Doyle was nominated for Best Director, Cynthia Erivo won Best Actress, and *The Color Purple* won Best Revival of a Musical. For his part, Doyle's explanation of its critical success is simpler: "I wanted to get what I love in the book."

In my next two experiences of the musical, in Philadelphia in December 2017, and then again a year later and closer to home at the Paper Mill Playhouse in Milburn, New Jersey, Celie was played by the formidable actress Adrianna Hicks. The absence of the magnetic Erivo enabled me to focus on things that I originally ignored. This time, I paid attention to the movement of the chairs themselves, which strangely made the set feel both sparse and more fully alive. Of them, Doyle said, "The chairs of course are multipurpose. And there's just something about having them on the big wall. The enormity of the wall was about power as well. Male power."

Two months after #MeToo went viral in 2018, however, I thought that the musical minimized the sexual trauma that Celie endured. Unlike the book, or even the movie, *The Color Purple* musical has always started with Celie's description of her stepfather's raping of her and then jumps quickly to the birth of her children. (In the Broadway original, a chorus of women humorously chant, "Who the daddy?" and in the revival a bedsheet is used.) As I sat there this time, I was annoyed by the muting of first Pa's and then Mister's violence, wondering if the story that had so graphically and realistically retold the horror of sexual violence—Celie's and mine—was now lost in the very moment of #MeToo that it had helped birth. At the end of the evening, the mainly white crowd stood roaring with relief and appreciation. I, however, clapped begrudgingly, feeling that somehow *The Color Purple* had betrayed me and the #MeToo movement before us.

I held on to that feeling for a long time. And wondered if *The Color Purple* had peaked and its message—or at least in its most ubiquitous form, as a musical—had lost its edge in our age of disclosure and newfound accountability. The audiences whom I saw the show with were mainly late baby boomers for whom Walker's original story might still seem startling, but I imagined that would not be the case for millennials, for whom gender and sexual fluidity are not abstract concepts but often a hard-fought reality of their lives and self-fashioning. To test out my theory, that summer, I hosted a series of conversations with high school girls about to leave for college who had read Walker's novel when they were in middle school or early high school but had not seen either the movie or the musical. These girls were introduced to me by their mothers or teachers, black and white women who had read *The Color Purple* as their own rite of passage but did not feel it necessary to discuss with their daughters. In one such gathering, Edie, a white eighteen-year-old graduate from Brooklyn on the eve of her matriculation to Yale, told me that what had always stood out to her was what Scott Sanders said drew him to the story as well: Walker's radical rendering of Celie forgiving

Albert. "In the age of MeToo, if you're just hearing Celie's story being told in the musical, it would be hard to get on board with forgiving Mister because what he did was so awful. I think, in the novel, because of the way it's written and because of who Celie is, it's less difficult than it would be," she said to us. "I've found, in the discussions that I have with people now, where I try to introduce complexity, people are afraid of it because no one knows how to deal. What if you have this relationship with this man even though he's done all these things?"

She concluded, "I think, overall, MeToo is doing an amazing thing, because it's bringing to light a system of oppression that was pushed under the rug in so many professions. I also think because now that all these terrible things have been exposed, no one knows how to deal with those gray areas and the middle ground. I think that's why the novel is important now." Admitting that I hadn't really thought much of what Albert—rather than the triad of Walker's women who had inspired me—meant in the age of #MeToo, I left slightly bewildered and amused; maybe I was wrong about the musical, and Mister, after all.

Seeing the musical again—for the fourth time—I mainly paid attention to Albert, a figure who often recedes in the background, despite being the progenitor of so much harm and heartbreak in Celie's life. When Shug and Celie leave him, his descent into madness is swift and relentless, enabling us to better visualize Walker's severe critique of patriarchy and Albert's reliance on it than we could with the novel or the movie. Just as Sofia and Harpo are the love story that we most cheer for, Albert, next to Celie, is the character whose transformation is the most far-reaching, and thus the most utopian. In his final scene alone at a picnic with Celie, Albert misreads Celie's affection and tolerance for him and proposes to her. And though I laughed at Albert's naïveté here, his tenderness and his transformation are real. Sharing a seashell with Celie, Albert tells her of his unfulfilled dreams of seeing the ocean. And while in the novel Walker wrote, "The more I wonder, the more I love," the musical's subtle change to the more pluralistic "The more us wonder, the more us love" marks Albert's newfound communion with Celie, with his family, and perhaps even with God herself.

"Albert gets his redemption and he does something," Doyle says. "He does things for the children of the community and maybe that's all a little through a pink gauze. But there's something wonderful about that. It's not to forgive Mister, but it's hard to break how you were raised. And of course that violence, as you know, really comes out of slavery." This time, as I watched Albert evolve and develop onstage, I wondered if Edie was right.

I've long fantasized about the moment when the men who raped me ask for my forgiveness. I've replayed the scene so many times: a sudden phone call, a random Facebook message, or an old-school letter replaying the night of my attack from my vantage point but now in their own words. Occasionally, I've tried to trace the fates of my assailants—the first, now a doctor living in Texas; the second, whose last name I am still not entirely certain of and whose face has partly receded from my memory—to see if their single act against my body has shaped their lives as much as it has mine. In my make-believe scenario, their apologies come with weeping, mine and theirs, for taking so much from me for so long. Their long-overdue confession delivered and somehow my closure is complete. The reality, however, is that like most rape survivors, I'm likely to never have such an opportunity. As such, I have time and time again learned to fill my own voids and violations with a tenderness that I've made for myself and have found in others.

In lieu of such accountability for my trauma, I have Mister. But he, more than any other of Walker's characters from *The Color Purple*, though inspired by her grandfather, remains completely fictional to me. This is not because I do not believe in Albert's redemption; it is because after millions of survivors of sexual assault and harassment have come forward in the past four years, the legal consequences have only impacted a couple of powerful men, like Harvey Weinstein and Bill Cosby, while only scores of others, like Matt Lauer, Louis C.K., and Al Franken, have experienced career humiliation. Against that backdrop, Albert's atonement appears even more subversive and elusive because he embarks on the journey knowing that such a promising ending is neither simple nor guaranteed. Instead of playing the victim, Albert owns his violence and the harm that he's caused.

In the last moments of the musical *The Color Purple*, Alice saw an ending on the Broadway stage that she always wanted on-screen: Albert, not set apart and forced to watch his family gathered together without him, but standing firmly with the blended family he helped reunite. He is not a hero—that status belongs to Celie, Shug, and Sofia—but his atonement is the wish fulfillment of every rape survivor I've ever met. In this way, Walker's novel still remains far ahead of its time, and ours, for while most of us survivors will never hear such an apology or benefit from such restitution, I now look to Albert for what could *be* rather than what was for me.

EPILOGUE:
NOW FEELING LIKE HOME

ON FRIDAY, JULY 12, 2019, a group of us—Mickalene, Scheherazade, Beverly, Evelyn White (Alice's biographer), director Pratibha Parmar and her partner, Shaheen Haq, who also helped produce Pratibha's 2013 documentary, *Alice Walker: Beauty in Truth*, and I—arrived at a six-bedroom condo on Lake Oconee, an hour southeast of Atlanta. Developed in 1979 by the Georgia Power Company, Lake Oconee is a reservoir that powers a nearby hydroelectric plant. Its coasts are lined with golf courses, vacation homes, villa rentals, and a Ritz-Carlton. Drawn to its simple shoreline and closeness to Eatonton, Alice had just closed on a cottage there. Lake Oconee, named after the Okonee people of the Creek nation, resonated with Walker. But even more compelling was the fact that this lake did not exist when she was a child. As such, unlike Eatonton's nearby vestiges, like the public library, elementary school, and town hall, it was not a reminder of the South's ugly, Jim Crow past. By signing her name on the deed, Alice intervened and interrupted the cycle of economic exploitation and intergenerational trauma that defined her family's relationship to the land here for well over a century.

Almost a full year after my first trip to Eatonton, the town looked significantly different. Local stores dressed their windows in purples and lavenders in honor of "Alice Walker 75," a day-long, county-wide celebration of Putnam County's most beloved artist, hosted by the local Georgia Writers' Museum and Valerie Boyd, the Hurston biographer and editor of the forthcoming *Gathering Blossoms Under Fire: The Journals of Alice Walker*. The closed-down Pex movie theater, at which Alice saw *Song of the South* and her mother watched *The Color Purple,* had proudly displayed, "Happy Birthday, Alice Walker" on its marquee. Flags with Alice's name were everywhere in the town's center. The Plaza Arts Center that Beverly, Valerie, and I visited in 2018 no longer exhibited watercolor paintings of Uncle Remus by a local artist throughout its building. Now, its walls were adorned with sculptures, collages, and paintings on migration, longing, and the African Diaspora by Atlanta artists Maurice Evans and Grace Kisa. Most impressively, the formerly empty auditorium seats were filled to the brim with seniors and teens, travelers, and tourists. A multiracial crowd who still felt connected to Walker and once upon a time lost themselves in her words.

"I'm so happy looking at all of us," Alice said from the stage to the audience, which included her family sitting in the front row. "When Rebecca's father and I went to Mississippi, it was to create this. To sit together and listen to beautiful music and poetry together without embarrassment, without shame," Walker said, speaking on her and Mel's years as young civil rights activists. "Many people made the ultimate sacrifice, but we felt it was worth it. Every day we saw incredible heroism and love. It was all for this. So, this is a homecoming to a place that is now feeling like home."

Wearing dark khaki pants, a canary-yellow shirt, and a blue-and-silver-striped silk wrap, Alice bowed slightly at us, concluding her remarks by crossing her arms over her heart. From my own spiritual practice, I recognized her arm gesture to be a variation on the Buddhist mudra, *vajrapradama*, a sign to indicate a transferring of peaceful energy from one person to another. In English, the Sanskrit word is often translated as "self-confidence," a feeling that I once thought when meeting Alice for the first time had come naturally to her. But, as I wrote this book, I realized she had earned it the hard way, by overcoming and outlasting controversies that encircled her. Each embroilment, starting with the early criticism that she had colluded with Gloria Steinem and Steven Spielberg in violently stereotyping black men in *The Color Purple*; to the abuse she endured for her indictment of female genital mutilation in Africa in *Possessing the Secret of Joy*, her 1992 novel that featured Celie's daughter-in-law, Tashi, and her and Pratibha's documentary (and book) *Warrior Marks* from the early-1990s; to the more recent accusations of anti-Semitism as a result of her naming British conspiracy theorist David Icke's *And the Truth Shall Set You* as an entry for "By the Book," a weekly feature in the *New York Times Book Review*, all stereotyped her as a black woman filled with hate and consumed by anger. The image of her that emerges in these conflicts is always unrecognizable to those closest to her, and in direct odds with the themes of love, forgiveness, and redemption that dominate her oeuvre, and which have healed millions along the way.

In December 2018, Nylah Burton, a black Jewish writer, published an essay on *New York* magazine's website about Walker and the Icke controversy. Describing her first encounter with *The Color Purple*, Burton wrote, "I was drawn to it because it was haunted by ghosts—the ghosts of Alice Walker's past." Later, Burton continued, "Eloquently and bravely, she was able to confront generational trauma by telling a universal tale that still felt faithful to her own story. And it was Walker's ability to throw open the shutters and allow her ghosts—our ghosts—into her writing that made it so revelatory." By the end of her fraught essay on what she perceives as Walker's vexed relationship with Judaism, Burton declared that she could not give up on the novel nor cancel it, making little distinction between Walker herself and Walker's prose. Ultimately, the disruptive power of *The Color Purple* still holds, attracting praise and attack in equal measure, even now. Alice's unvarnished truth remains her unique gift to the world. That her truth continues to be an unsettling experience is what made *The Color Purple* such a powerful book in the first place.

I didn't see ghosts in Eatonton, just ancestors. During our trip there, Mickalene, Scheherazade, and I drove to Alice's family cemetery. Retracing the same path that I took with Beverly and Valerie the year before, I directed our car to Wards Chapel A.M.E. Church, then we walked across the street to Walker's family plot. The first thing I noticed was that the ground had been moved. In preparation for the celebration, the grass had been cut, and flowers placed on the gravestones. And in my search for *The Color Purple*, I realized that I had also changed, with a deeper connection to Walker's past and the family members of hers that sprang to life as characters in her award-winning novel. Now, when I saw Willie Lee's tombstone, I heard Harpo's laugh. I imagined Sofia's strut as I stood near Minnie Lou's final bed. At Henry Clay's granite slab, I saw Albert's longing for Shug. And as I stared at Rachel's gravesite, I paused and lingered over her name, wishing that she had experienced the beloved community that Alice had gifted Celie *and* us.

Her words invited black women sexual assault survivors into a gathering space in which we are believed and comforted—not just by each other but by our friends and families. The logical extension of her vision was always to help our country, and our world, understand the ways in which our fates are linked and tethered to the vulnerability of black women and children and the violence done against us, something that we are all charged to prevent. Through Celie, Alice Walker created a template for those of us who dare say that we've been raped by someone we trusted. Her most famous novel is a touchstone for any artist who helped us speak our truth to the world.

It is safe to say that without *The Color Purple*, Oprah would not have felt empowered to tell the story of hundreds of rape victims on-air, thus destigmatizing such trauma for millions. Scheherazade might not have picked up her camera to photograph my journey of healing after being raped twice in college, and we definitely would not have had the courage to start A Long Walk Home and help thousands of survivors heal. Aishah Shahidah Simmons might not have directed *NO! The Rape Documentary*, on rape in the black community. dream hampton might not have taken on the Lifetime docu-series *Surviving R. Kelly*. Tarana Burke might not have founded the #MeToo movement. And though each of us has had to confront our fair share of critics and censors, we did not have to pay Alice's price of being a pioneer. Even in her loneliest moments following the fallout of *The Color Purple*, Alice gave us another model: out of our pain, we could make art. Through our forgiveness, a new family could be born.

And so, new friendships are made, new sisterhoods are formed. On our last night in Eatonton, Mickalene, Scheherazade, and I sat in the third row at the Plaza Arts Center as "Alice Walker 75" came to an end. The prodigal daughter had danced at her own party and made her own pilgrimage. We, her readers and artistic daughters, paid homage and healed. The wounds of Eatonton's racial past and how those harms haunt our present were eased by Walker's ability to gather such a diverse group in a town once so painfully divided by the color line. In the final minutes of the event, Valerie, in conversation with Alice onstage, asked her a favor: "Do you mind reading a section from *The Color Purple*?"

With tears in my eyes and a smile so full and bright, I realized that in all my life, I'd actually never heard Alice Walker say Celie's words out loud in person. "I'm not wearing my reading glasses, so that may be an issue, but I should know this by heart," she laughingly said. "'Dear Nettie.' And Nettie, by the way, was my grandmother's name—Nettie Grant—so this person is named after her, she died when I was two."

She continued, "'I don't write to God no more, I write to you.'"

AFTERWORD
BY BEVERLY GUY-SHEFTALL

DEAR ALICE:

When Professor Tillet (Salamishah) asked me to write the afterword to her book, I decided to respond with an open letter to you rather than the conventional expository text. I wanted to celebrate the epistolary genre that you so brilliantly mastered in *The Color Purple*.

Alice . . . wise, free, gentle, fierce, passionate, courageous . . . I am grateful for the gift of your friendship, your persistent resistance to injustice, and the stunning artistry of your life and writings.

1961: Atlanta, Georgia, your first year at Spelman College. I would join you a year later. You were inspired by Martin Luther King Jr. and Coretta Scott King, whom you met for the first time during your first year at Spelman, at her home prior to your attending the World Youth Peace Festival in Helsinki. Not many of us were aware then of Coretta's long history as a peace activist, which began when she was a student at Antioch College. I am happy you included your essay "Coretta King: Revisited" in your collection of essays, *In Search of Our Mothers' Garden: Womanist Prose*, as well as your praise-song, "Choice: A Tribute to Dr. Martin Luther King, Jr.," in which you recall having seen him on television in 1960, when Hamilton Holmes and Charlayne Hunter were the first African Americans to desegregate the University of Georgia.

As a frequent visitor to Dexter Avenue Baptist Church in Montgomery, Alabama, when I visited my mother's sister and her family, I also witnessed King's Sunday sermons. Your words captured his impact on me as well: "At the moment I first saw him, he was being handcuffed and shoved into a police truck . . . He displayed no fear, but seemed calm and serene, unaware of his own extraordinary courage. His whole body, like his conscience, was at peace. At the moment I saw his resistance, I knew I would never be able to live in this country without resisting everything that sought to disinherit me, and I would never be forced away from the land of my birth without a fight."

You were taught by Professor Howard Zinn, who in his "open letter" to the Spelman Board of Trustees, faculty, students and alumni, and President Manley upon his dismissal from the College in 1963, quoted your student essay from his class on the Soviet Union that previous semester. You concluded your paper "On Djilas and Kolakowski" by noting that "Every country should have a Kolakowski, someone who questions the unanswerable, but who nevertheless prods the people into thinking before they act." But it is the last sentence of Zinn's "open letter," with his closing words about you and all the Spelman women that you represented, that left its readers with one of the most precious memories a teacher could have: "A student who thinks and writes like this deserves nothing but the best."

It is likely that Zinn and your Spelman "sisters," including me, were unaware of your history growing up in Eatonton, Georgia, and had not experienced "the best." In "Lest We Forget: An

Open Letter to My Sisters Who Are Brave," which you circulated on March 21, 2008, to several of us (forty-five years after Zinn's "open letter") in the midst of the Barack Obama/Hillary Clinton race for the Democratic nomination, you described the dehumanizing world of Jim and Jane Crow, which was also familiar to me, even though I was born in 1946 in urban Memphis, Tennessee. When you reflected upon the historic election that would result in the first Black president, you shared what you wanted for the country and what I also wanted, and remembered your influential teacher:

> I want a grown-up attitude toward Cuba, a country and a people I love; I want an end to the embargo that has harmed my friends and their children, children, who, when I visit Cuba, trustingly turn their faces up for me to kiss. I agree with a teacher of mine, Howard Zinn, that war is as objectionable as cannibalism and slavery; it is beyond obsolete as a means of improving life. I want an end to the on-going war immediately, and I want the soldiers to be encouraged to destroy their weapons and to drive themselves out of Iraq. I want the Israeli government to be made accountable for its behavior toward the Palestinians, and I want the people of the United States to cease acting like they don't understand what is going on. All colonization, all occupation, all repression basically looks the same, whoever is doing it.

Three years later, in June 2011, when I joined an indigenous and women of color delegation to the occupied territories of Palestine, I thought about your bravery (in words and deeds) and remembered sharing my experiences with you at your home near Philo, California. I still remember your attentive smile as I described one of the most transformative weeks of my adult life. I felt that the sisterly bond between us for nearly fifty years had been strengthened, and that we would remember that afternoon on your couch at Temple Jook for a very long time.

1970: I haven't seen you since you left Spelman at the end of your sophomore year for Sarah Lawrence College in 1967. I am teaching English at Alabama State University, a year before I returned to Spelman's English department in 1971. During that momentous year, I read your first novel, *The Third Life of Grange Copeland*, Toni Morrison's *The Bluest Eye* (the first two novels by black women writers that I began teaching at Spelman), and Toni Cade Bambara's *The Black Woman*. I didn't know it at the time, but while you were teaching a course on black women writers at the University of Massachusetts Boston in 1972 (a year before you taught the course at Wellesley College), I began to teach a mini-course on black women writers in our department of english. Years later, Barbara Smith, co-editor of *But Some of Us Are Brave*, shared your syllabus with me when I visited her at Simmons College to talk about my ideas about establishing a Women's Center at Spelman.

I, along with my departmental colleague Roseann P. Bell, were determined, after reading your novel and Morrison's, to make visible the critically important but largely invisible black women's literary tradition that began in the mid-nineteenth century. The result was *Sturdy Black Bridges: Visions of Black Women in Literature*, the first anthology of black women's writing, which was published by Doubleday in 1979. When the first draft of

Bridges was completed in 1976, you had, over the previous decade, published two volumes of poetry, a collection of short stories, and two novels.

Because of your extraordinary impact on African American letters and young black women, when we approached Mary Helen Washington, a pioneering critic, she submitted the insightful and loving "Essay on Alice Walker," the subject of her doctoral dissertation. In her opening sentences of a lengthy essay, she captured your genius: "It is clear that the special identifying mark of her writing is her concern for the lives of black women . . . [H]er main preoccupation has been the souls of black women."

I read from cover to cover the first issue of *Ms.* magazine in July 1972 and became a lifetime subscriber. Perhaps the most impactful on me and countless other black women was your now canonical essay "In Search of Our Mothers' Gardens: The Creativity of Black Women in the South," which appeared in the May 1974 issue. I read "In Search of Zora Neale Hurston" in the 1975 issue and your second novel, *Meridian*, a year later. When you were on the 1982 cover of *Ms.* magazine (the fiction issue), I was determined to read *The Color Purple*; I saw the controversial Spielberg-directed movie in 1985, and attended the mesmerizing world premiere of the musical adaptation at the Alliance Theater with you and friends in 2004, and a year later on Broadway in New York.

Throughout our celebrations of your remarkable literary achievements, it would have been impossible to imagine the venom that would be unleashed surrounding the publication and film release of *The Color Purple*. I read with deep sadness the scathing reviews by black men and women, critics and laypeople alike. Over coffee, at conferences, and in living rooms and classrooms, I also was buoyed by conversations among black women who spoke about the truths you had dared to make visible.

When I pondered which writing of yours I wanted to include in *Words of Fire: An Anthology of African-American Feminist Thought* (first published in 1995), I recalled your counterdiscourse on "womanism", which had provided alternative terminology for black feminists during a time when many women of color were raising angry voices about their marginalization or erasure within mainstream white feminist discourse. But I settled finally on "In the Closet of the Soul," because it provided a passionate counterargument to those angry voices within the black community in particular who had raged against *Purple* because of its so-called negative treatment of black men, its incest theme, and embrace of lesbian love. The essay was originally a letter you wrote in 1986 in response to a question about your reaction to criticisms of the character Mister, whom you tell us you deeply love, certainly not for his brutality and oppression of women, but because "he went deeply enough into himself to find the courage to change. To grow."

I wanted you to have the last word in *Words of Fire* because you capture, eloquently and succinctly and unapologetically, why we must commit to feminist/womanist liberation, in words and deeds, and without fail: "It has been black men (as well as black women and Native Americans) who have provided in this culture the most inspiring directions for everyone's freedom. As a daughter of these men, I did not hear a double standard when they urged each person to struggle to be free, even if they intended to impart one. When Malcolm said, 'Freedom, by any means necessary,' I thought I knew what he meant. When Martin said, 'Agitate nonviolently against unjust oppression,' I assumed he also meant in the home, if that's where the oppression was. When Frederick Douglass talked about not expecting crops without first plowing up the ground, I felt he'd noticed the weeds in most of our backyards. It is nearly CRUSHING to realize there was an assumption on ANYONE's part that black women would not fight injustice except when the foe was white."

Here we are.

Fifty-eight years since I met you with our memories, our stories, our hopes, and our knowing that anything you love can be saved.

Over thirty books, including a Pulitzer Prize, you are beloved here and around the globe for your writing, your activism, your unrelenting commitment to justice, and for always being yourself. You are a gift, Alice, to the universe because of your wisdom, truth-telling, generosity, reverence for the earth and all its inhabitants, and your deep knowing about what we need to do to keep ourselves and our communities healthy and whole. Even in the midst of toxic realities (war, poverty, racism, genocide, violence against women, cruelty to children and animals), you have never lost faith in the idea that "anything we love can be saved." On our campuses, we teach your poetry and novels and essays, craft Alice Walker seminars, call your name, share with students your journeys to Brooklyn, Boonville, Rwanda, the Congo, Gaza, and home to Eatonton, Georgia.

Salamishah Tillet's *In Search of The Color Purple* is a gift to the universe that painstakingly, meticulously, and lovingly describes all there is to know about the evolution of the novel, its characters, and its adaptation for film and the stage. It is a personal testimony to its healing properties and how it saved and helped to shape Salamishah's journey to wholeness. It beckons your critics to revisit their own rage and the sadness it generated.

I hope black women's suffering is made more legible in the retelling of the story of your "masterpiece."

What I know for sure is our evolving bonds, our sisterhood . . . with Gloria, Valerie, Ti, Salamishah, Scheherazade, Mickalene, and Racquel . . . were sparked by you! We love Celie and Shug and Sofia and Nettie and, of course, *The Color Purple*!

In struggle and joy,

Beverly

ACKNOWLEDGMENTS

When I began doing research for this book in March 2018, I could not imagine how much the conversation around sexual assault and harassment would change in just six months. The emergence of #MeToo as a movement that enabled millions of sexual assault victims to come forward was unparalleled; that many of these people were believed first by each other, and then by so many others, including individuals and industries that have long swept these forms of violence under the rug, was unprecedented. Whether this moment will flourish or be as inclusive as it needs to be remains uncertain. What has been made clear, however, is that hope has been released and, for a few, justice meted out. And for a small window of time, the work that my sister, Scheherazade, and I have been doing on behalf of thousands of black women and girls who have survived rape, like our mother, like myself, for the last twenty years with our organization, A Long Walk Home, has found a new voice and urgency in this moment. In this way, *In Search of* The Color Purple extends a conversation that I am already in as well as gently explores my journey to become a rape survivor who has learned to live without shame.

I often refer to this book as a gift. And like the best of gifts, it was unexpected and right on time. I have so many places and people to thank for its possibility. First, I'd like to thank the

University of Pennsylvania and Rutgers University–Newark for supporting my research (both archival and in person) for this book. I'd like to thank the archivists at the Rose Library at Emory University, where Alice Walker's extensive papers are held, for their patience and diligence. I'd like to thank Lucy McKeon and Madeleine Schwartz of the *New York Review of Books* for encouraging me to interview Alice for their online publication in 2018; that trip was the beginning of a fortuitous relationship. And to sisters Nadine and Jacqueline Mattis of Easton's Nook for nurturing my mind and nourishing my spirit.

This book simply would not be without Gloria Steinem, who first wrote to Alice when I agreed to do the book, and my feminist fairy godmothers Beverly Guy-Sheftall and Valerie Boyd, who not only took me on a road trip to Eatonton, Georgia, on a hot August afternoon but provided me with so much crucial information about *The Color Purple* that they are really the shadow writers of this book. Together, this trio reaffirmed my faith in feminist labor and of course women's friendship. Through this process, I have also made new friends: people who have been brought together by the magical healing properties of Walker's words. Thank you, John Legend, for introducing me to Quincy Jones, and thank you, Quincy Jones, for granting me an interview. Deep gratitude to RaMell Ross for connecting me with the most admirable Danny Glover. I owe much to Nicole Nichols for arranging for me and Oprah Winfrey to meet and for introducing me to Scott Sanders. What an honor it was to be granted so much time with Oprah Winfrey; we all are indebted to her for the work she has done and continues to do for rape victims everywhere. Scott Sanders is such a wonderful and generative new presence in my life, a true connector; I'm also grateful to him and John Doyles for talking to me about the various musical versions of *The Color Purple*. To Laurie Abraham and Edie Abraham-Macht—thanks for opening your home and yours hearts to me.

There are communities that help shape and sustain our creativity and our hearts. Fortunately, I am a member of a select few. My friendships with my mentors Farah Griffin, Thadious Davis, and Henry Louis Gates Jr. remain enduring springs of wisdom and compassion. To my former students Samuel Mondrey-Cohen, Mimi Owusu, Victoria Ford, John Howard, Kaneesha Parsard, Ryan Jobson, and Brandon Terry, thanks for your kindness. Dagmawi Woubshet, Soyica Colbert, GerShun Avilez, Marcus Hunter, and Regine Jean-Charles, you make this academic journey so much more meaningful and endlessly worthwhile. From my old home of Penn: so happy for John Jackson, Deborah Thomas, Guthrie Ramsey, Zachary Lesser, and Taije Silverman. A special shout-out to my former graduate students and research assistants for this project: Julia Cox and Elias Rodriques. At my new home of Rutgers–Newark, I've been lucky to be surrounded by colleagues who inspire me daily: Nancy Cantor, John Keene, Jessica Hernandez, Rigoberto Gonzalez, Belinda Edmondson, Ann Englot, Mark Krasovic, Fran Bartkowski, Sherri-Ann Butterfield, Amber Randolph, Peter Englot, Mehreen Mian, Anthony Alvarez, Jacquie Mattis, Christina Strasburger, and Jordan Casteel. Special thanks to Jim Goodman for his thoughtfulness and the invitation to his Writing History workshop, and to Laura Troiano and Alliyah Allen for their hard work helping me with all the minute details that went into this book. It was lovely to spend time with you both in Eatonton and I'm truly grateful for your support. To my newest yet feels-like-a-lifetime friends: Nick Kline—what would I do without our dreaming, strategizing, and making-art-that-matters sessions? And Melissa Cooper—who knew that Obert Clark Tanner would give us a lifetime of laughs, love, and premonitions?

Paul Farber, Aaron Skyrpski, and Iggy, our family friendships are one of the most cherished parts of my life. To Jessica Garz, thanks for your goodness in all things, and to Elizabeth Mendez Berry, thanks for your kindness and vulnerability. To the Bawse Ladies—Sayu Bhojwani, Karla Monterroso, Carmen Rojas, and Alex Bernadotte, and our original one, Sarah Peter—thanks for reminding me that with generosity and sisterhood, we remain on the right side of all things good and just. To my sisters in the struggle: Pamela Shifman, Sarah Jones, Ai-jen Poo, Fatima Gross-Graves, Cidra Sebastien, Tarana Burke, Jennifer Parker, Beth Ritchie, Cathy Cohen, Aishah Shahidah Simmons, and Joanne Smith, thank you for making the world a lot more safe and free for us all. To the BMJs, especially Lisa Davis, Keisha Jeremie, Klancy Miller, Tiffany Dufu, Zuhairah Washington, and Yetta Banks, thanks for all your support and dreaming of the moment beyond. To the following crews: Asare-Jean-Charles, Walker-Ritchie, Mendez Berry-Graham, the Streaters, Levene-Harvell, Clark-Soares, Miller-Russell, I can't imagine a better group with whom I could do this journey of doing it "all"; you all make up the most glorious lemons in my lemonade.

To those who've made this book better in all the ways that matter. My original writing partner, Dawn Lundy Martin, thanks for checking in, your feedback, and timely insights. Mickalene Thomas is a goddess-send and I am so happy Beverly and Celie and Shug completed our circle of sisterhood. To Kamilah Forbes, who daily helped me plot out this book and helped me believe that I belong in "Authorville," even without the requisite carousel umbrella.

To my A Long Walk Home family: Connie Harvey, Trina Greene Brown, Leah Gipson, Tiffany Johnson, Danielle Nolan, Rachel Kelsey, Lanesha Baldwin, Marline Johnson, Aja Reynolds, Maureen Jackson, Candance Averyhart, Linda Carlson, Corey Harris, Ika Martinez, Chloe Wayne, Asia Willis, Paul, Regine, and Elizabeth; our *Story of a Rape Survivor* cast and crew: Ugochi Nwaogwugwu, Patrice McClean, Hettie Barnhill, Rachel Walker, Logan Vaughn, Jean-René Rinvil, Yvonne Shirley, Robin Shanae, and Tonya Lewis Lee and Cindi Leive; to countless other youth leaders, their parents and families, and survivors who have shared their stories with me—thank you for your activism, your art, and for helping me believe in the world again.

Thanks to Abrams Press and my editor, Jamison Stoltz, for his care, patience, and delight, and for indulging me by changing his schedule at the last minute to see *The Color Purple* with me on a random night in a Village movie theater.

Thanks to my mother-in-law, Marilyn Strickland, for whom I hope I've done the South well and who gave me crucial time to create. To my aunt Felicia Phillip, who shared so much to help reshape this story. To my therapist, Jane Abrams, for always helping me see the trees. To our caregiver, Marissa Rangel, for easing my mind so I can write.

Thanks to my mother, Volora Howell, from whom I first learned the spirit of "black feminism" and who gave me my first library—two priceless gifts that made all the difference in my world. And to my father, Lennox Tillet, whose optimism and compassion taught me the act of forgiveness.

Thanks to my brother, Shaka Davis, whose life and too-early death always gave me more purpose and whom I'll forever miss.

To my children, Seneca Steplight-Tillet and Sidney Steplight-Tillet, thanks for your beauty, boldness, and bravery and for making our world better and far brighter than I knew without you. To my life partner, Solomon Steplight, my debt to you is as eternal as my love for you.

To my agent, Tanya McKinnon, who never wavered in her belief in me since we met on that winter day at Sarabeth's, thank you for helping me own my "voice" as a writer, a mother, and a black feminist intellectual.

And to my sister, Scheherazade Tillet, you, like Alice, have helped so many people heal. I can't thank you enough for helping me find my way home.

NOTES

1. THE LOVELINESS OF HER SPIRIT

1 "all you can see": Alice Walker, interview with the author, September 18, 2018.

2 a typical show might make: Gordon Cox, "Tuners Trumpet Their Trinkets," *Variety*, December 31, 2006, https://variety.com/2006/legit/news/tuners-trumpet-their-trinkets-1117956437/.

2 they'd ask her: Alice Walker, "Writing *The Color Purple*," in *In Search of Our Mothers' Gardens: Womanist Prose* (New York: Harvest, 1983), 356.

2 "a good place to live": Evelyn White, *Alice Walker: A Life* (New York: Norton, 2004), 312.

3 "winding away": Robert M. Anderson, *Boonville* (New York: Perennial, 2003), 1.

3 "haltingly, to speak": Walker, "Writing *The Color Purple*," 357.

4 "happening to me": Alice Walker, *The Color Purple* (New York: Harcourt Brace Jovanovich, 1982), 1.

5 "Do You Know What Rape Feels Like": Salamishah Tillet, "Do You Know What Rape Feels Like," in A Long Walk Home's *Story of a Rape Survivor* (1999).

8 "self-revelation": Zora Neale Hurston, *Their Eyes Were Watching God*, foreword by Mary Helen Washington and an afterword by Henry Louis Gates Jr. (1937; New York: HarperPerennial, 1999), 6.

9 "emotion one feels": Alice Walker, "Looking for Zora," in *In Search of Our Mothers' Gardens*, 115.

9 "self-revelation": Henry Louis Gates Jr., *The Signifying Monkey: A Theory of Afro-American Literary Criticism* (New York: Oxford University Press, 1988), 245.

9 "novelistic daughter": Harold Bloom, *Alice Walker* (New York: Chelsea House Books, 2007), 1.

12 "majority white Hollywood": Jacqueline Bobo, "Black Women's Responses to *The Color Purple*," *Jump Cut* 33 (Feb. 1988): 43–51.

12 "like Mister": Larry Rohter, "Spike Lee Makes His Movie," *New York Times*, August 10, 1986, 14.

13 Alice Walker Literary Society: "Interview with Rudolph Byrd," in *The Color Purple: A Memory Book of the Broadway Musical*, ed. Lise Funderburg, Alice Walker, and Brenda Russell (New York: Carroll & Graf, 2006), 25.

13 "most hated black woman in America": Beverly Guy-Sheftall, interview with the author, November 1, 2019.

13 "what become of them": Alice Walker, "Journal Entry," December 13, 1986, in *The Same River Twice: Honoring the Difficult* (New York: Washington Square Press, 2006), 280.

14 "in which I was raised": Alice Walker, "This Was Not an Area of Large Plantations: Suffering Too Insignificant for the Majority to See," in *We Are the Ones We Have Been Waiting For: Inner Light in a Time of Darkness* (New York: New Press, 2006), 88–110.

14 "a book about God": Alice Walker, "Tsunamis and Hurricanes: Twenty-five Years After Publishing *The Color Purple*," in *The Color Purple*, 25th Anniversary Edition (London: Weidenfeld and Nicolson, 2007): ix–xv.

19 "looking at reality": Elena Featherston, "Alice Walker on Alice Walker," *San Francisco Focus*, December 1985, 96.

24 Broadway revival of the musical: Alice Walker and Verdecia M. García, *Taking the Arrow Out of the Heart: Poems* (New York: 37 Ink/Atria Books, 2018), 19–23.

25 "six days a week": Cynthia Erivo Performs "I'm Here" from *The Color Purple* at the MAKERS Conference, Terranea Resort, Rancho Palos Verdes, CA, April 4, 2007. https://www.youtube.com/watch?v=E-Flmo07ddk

27 "he was drunk": Walker, *The Same River Twice*, 211.

27 "two can play at this game": White, *Alice Walker*, 19.

28 "heartaches and revelations": Walker, "Writing *The Color Purple*," 356.

29 "Ma-Ma's life": White, *Alice Walker*, 335.

30 "freedom to thrive": Alice Walker, "To the Cuban Reader," December 2013, https://alicewalkersgarden.com/2014/01/now-is-the-time-to-open-your-heart-to-the-cuban-reader/.

32 "'cruel enough to stop the blood'": Alice Walker, "In Search of Our Mothers' Gardens," in *In Search of Our Mothers' Gardens*, 231–43.

32 picture of four women: *Grant, Nellie Lee, Minnie Lou Grant, "Miss Mary,"
    and Rachel* (photographer unknown), undated. (photographer unknown),
    undated, Alice Walker Archive, Emory University, box 194, folder 36.

34 "her spirit": Alice Walker, "*The Color Purple*: A Synopsis for Film," in *The
    Same River Twice*, 50–56.

34 Walker texted about Rachel: Alice Walker, electronic text message to the
    author, November 11, 2018.

2. I HAD TO DO A LOT OF OTHER WRITING
TO GET TO THIS POINT

38 "why write such a novel?": Alice Walker, *The Third Life of Grange Copeland*
    (1970; Orlando, FL: Harcourt, 2003), 314.

38 "my humiliation": Alice Walker, "Staying Home in Mississippi," *New York
    Times*, August 26, 1973.

39 "Young Ladies Who Can Picket": Howard Zinn, "Finishing School for
    Pickets," *Nation*, December 22, 2009.

39 "family farm in Eatonton, Georgia": Howard Zinn, *You Can't Be Neutral
    on a Moving Train: A Personal History of Our Times* (Boston: Beacon Press,
    1994), 44.

39 his duties with the college: Martin B. Duberman, *Howard Zinn: A Life on
    the Left* (New York: New Press, 2012).

40 "'I suppose'": Zinn, *You Can't Be Neutral on a Moving Train*, 43.

40 "'being buried alive'": White, *Alice Walker*, 92.

40 "'it was very hard'": White, *Alice Walker*, 111.

41 "'I was pregnant'" White, *Alice Walker*, 112.

42 "'not well again for a year'": Alice Walker, "Abortion," in *You Can't Keep
    a Good Woman Down: Stories* (New York: Harcourt Brace Jovanovich,
    1982), 68.

42 " 'Long Live the Klan'?": White, *Alice Walker*, 130.

43 "Such a cliché": Herbert Mitgang, "Alice Walker Recalls the Civil Rights
    Battle," *New York Times*, April 16, 1983, Section 1, page 13.

44 "I could not help it": Walker, *Third Life of Grange Copeland*, 314.

44 "from the light": Walker, *Third Life of Grange Copeland*, 161.

44 she concluded: Walker, *Third Life of Grange Copeland*, 315.

45 "any such domination": Walker, *In Search of Our Mothers' Gardens*, 344.

45 "the same": Walker, *Third Life of Grange Copeland*, 316.

45 "family saga spanning three generations": The Third of Grange Copeland, Kirkus Reviews, Aug. 1, 1970. Review posted online October 6, 2011: https://www.kirkusreviews.com/book-reviews/andre-bernard/third-life -of-grange-copeland/

45 "historical novel form": Kay Bourne, "Alice Walker's First Novel Hits Home," *Bay State Banner*, August 13, 1970.

45 "intense degradation": Victor A. Kramer, "Review of the Third Life," *Library Journal*, July 1970.

46 "too much to dissect it": Josephine Hendin, "Books for Young People (4 Reviews)," *Saturday Review*, August 22, 1970, 55–57.

46 "'they too often are'": White, *Alice Walker*, 189.

47 "American novelists now working": Sara Blackburn, "You Still Can't Go Home Again," *New York Times*, December 30, 1973.

47 "instead as sociology": Alice Walker, "Letters to the Editor," *New York Times*, January 20, 1974, 26.

49 "surrounded by black men": Alice Walker, *Meridian* (1976; New York: Harcourt, 2003), 175.

49 "enemies as comrades": Margo Jefferson, "Across the Barricades," *Newsweek*, May 31, 1976, 71.

50 "clearly the focus": Mel Watkins, "Some Letters Went to God," *New York Times*, July 25, 1982, 7:7.

50 white nor black critics: Alice Walker in Ray Anello and Pamela Abramson, "Characters in Search of a Book," *Newsweek*, June 21, 1982, 67.

50 "I work for the ancestors. Period": White, *Alice Walker*, 293.

3. IN THIS STRUGGLE LANGUAGE IS CRUCIAL

52 "First, language": John Ferrone, letter to Alice Walker, September 9, 1981, personal collection of Alice Walker.

53 "writing occurred in the past": Alice Walker, letter to John Ferrone, September 16, 1981, personal collection of Alice Walker.

55 "reserve for the climax": Peter S. Prescott, "A Long Road to Liberation," *Newsweek*, June 21, 1982, 67.

55 "her life itself": Alice Walker, "Coming In from the Cold: Welcoming the

Old, Funny-Talking Ancient Ones into the Warm Room of Present Consciousness, or, Natty Dread Rides Again!" in *Living by the Word: Selected Writings, 1973–1987* (San Diego: Harcourt Brace Jovanovich, 1990), 58. Walker read the essay at the National Writers Union in New York in spring 1984 and the Black Women's Forum in Los Angeles on November 17, 1984.

56 "historians of the future": Joel Chandler Harris, editorial, *Atlanta Constitution*, April 9, 1880.

57 "on television": Alice Walker, "Elethia," in *You Can't Keep a Good Woman Down*, 30.

57 "Uncle Remus stories": Alice Walker, "The Dummy in the Window: Joel Chandler Harris and the Invention of Uncle Remus," in *Living by the Word*, 29.

58 "Walt Disney": Walker, "The Dummy in the Window," 32.

58–59 "Harris's books in the foreground": See mural here: https://www.putnamdevelopmentauthority.com/wp-content/uploads/2017/04/Writers-Museum-Mural.jpg.

59 "By making me ashamed of it": Walker, "The Dummy in the Window," 32.

59 "our parents and grandparents": Walker, *In Search of Our Mothers' Gardens*, 84.

60 black oral tradition: Henry Louis Gates Jr., *The Signifying Monkey: A Theory of Afro-American Literary Criticism* (New York: Oxford University Press, 1988), 181.

60 "*formal* and textual way": Henry Louis Gates Jr., letter to Alice Walker, November 18, 1983, personal collection of Alice Walker.

62 "If only Tea Cake could make her certain!": Hurston, *Their Eyes Were Watching God*, 252.

62 "Her gift for poetic phrase": Alain Locke, review of Zora Neale Hurston's *Their Eyes Were Watching God*, *Opportunity*, June 1, 1938.

62 "white folks' laugh": Richard Wright, "Between Laughter and Tears," in *New Masses*, October 5, 1937, 22–23.

62 "myself—have!": Alice Walker, "Zora Neale Hurston: A Cautionary Tale and a Partisan View," in *In Search of Our Mothers' Gardens*, 86.

63 "dress just alike": Walker, *The Color Purple*, 13.

63 "Nettie. Yes, but Celie?": Audre Lorde, letter to Alice Walker, 1982, personal collection of Alice Walker.

64 "to speak her story": John F. Callahan, letter to Alice Walker, September 30, 1981, personal collection of Alice Walker.

64–65 "... we want 'poems that kill'": Amiri Baraka, "Black Art," in *The Norton Anthology of African American Literature*, ed. Henry Louis Gates Jr. and Nellie Y. McKay (1966; New York: W. W. Norton, 1996), 998.

4. OPENING THIS SECRET TO THE WORLD

69 stepped on barbed wire: Alice Walker, "Beauty: When the Other Dancer Is the Self," in *In Search of Our Mothers' Gardens*, 363.

70 "scandalous books": Walker, "Beauty: When the Other Dancer Is the Self," 367.

72 "intellectual's pinup": Leonard Levitt, "She: The Awesome Power of Gloria Steinem," *Esquire*, October 1971, 87–89, 200–205. For long article, see: https://classic.esquire.com/article/1971/10/1/she.

73 "into the world": Alice Walker, letter to John Ferrone, November 10, 1981, personal collection of Alice Walker.

73 "Also, Celie and Nettie and Shug": Gloria Steinem, letter to Alice Walker, October 25, 1981, personal collection of Alice Walker.

74 "diverse ethnic backgrounds": Gloria Steinem, "Alice Walker: Do You Know This Woman? She Knows You," *Ms.*, June 1982, 35–37, 89–94.

75 "the leader of the movement": White, *Alice Walker*, 269.

75 "I don't know": Cecil Brown and Toni Morrison, "Interview with Toni Morrison," *Massachusetts Review* 36, no. 3 (Autumn 1995): 455–73.

75 "controlling the ocean!": Gloria Steinem, email to Salamishah Tillet, May 9, 2019, personal collection of the author.

75 "Black men as rapists": Richard Gregory Lewis, "Depicting Struggle, Survival Is the Task for Alice Walker," *National Leader*, October 7, 1982, 18, 26.

76 feminist movement itself: Michele Wallace, "Black Macho and the Myth of the Superwoman, an Excerpt," *Ms.*, January 1979, 45–48, 87–89, 91.

77 "whites view us": Robert Staples, "The Myth of Black Macho: A Response to Angry Black Feminists," *Black Scholar* 10, no. 6/7 (March/April 1979): 24–33.

77 "it turns out": Gabby Bess, Revisiting Michele Wallace's Essential Black Feminist Text 'Black Macho,'" *Vice*, July 22, 2015, https://www.vice.com

/en_us/article/vdxya3/revisiting-michele-wallaces-essential-black-feminist -text-black-macho.

78 "lackluster and intrusive": Watkins, "Some Letters Went to God."

78 "ne'er-do-wells": Mel Watkins, "Sexism, Racism and Black Women Writers," *New York Times*, June 15, 1986, 7:1.

79 "permanent importance": Prescott, "A Long Road to Liberation," 67.

80 "black women in the 1940s": Megan Rosenfeld, "Profiles in Purple and Black," *Washington Post*, October 15, 1982.

80 sophomore in college in 1993: Ann Allen Shockley, *Loving Her* (New York: Avon Books, 1974).

80 "This bullshit should not be tolerated": Frank Lamont Phillips, "Review of *Loving Her*, by Ann Allen Shockley," *Black World*, September 1975, 89–90.

81 "ridiculed or obscured": Alice Walker, "A Daring Subject Boldly Shared," *Ms.*, April 1975, 120, 124.

82 "breakthrough in Black literature": Barbara Smith, "Sexual Oppression Unmasked," *Callaloo* 22 (Autumn 1984): 170–76.

82 "bias towards lesbianism": Richard Colvin, " 'Color Purple' OK with Committee," *Oakland Tribune*, June 22, 1984, B:1, 9.

82 "aesthetically beautiful way": Colvin, " 'Color Purple' OK with Committee."

83 "emulate her": David Bradley, "Novelist Alice Walker Telling the Black Woman's Story," *New York Times*, January 8, 1984, 6:24.

84 "It should have been about Bradley": Walker, *The Same River Twice*, 166.

84 "the achievements and identities of women": Miriam Rosenberg, "Letter to the Editor," *New York Times*, February 12, 1984, 6: 94.

84 "Maybe my feet are, too": Alice Walker, "Letter to the Editor of *The New York Times Magazine*," January 5, 1984, personal collection of Alice Walker.

84 "Just when I felt comfortable": Walker, *The Same River Twice*, 166.

85 "come straight through": Lee Bailey interview with Quincy Jones, "Interview with Quincy Jones," Warner Bros. Musical Show, Promotional Materials, February 1986. https://www.youtube.com/watch?v=hFJMqTK4c8w

85 "a secret dream of mine": "Quincy," dir. Rashida Jones and Alan Hicks, Netflix, September 21, 2018.

85 "our dreams in the movies too": Quincy Jones, *Q: The Autobiography of Quincy Jones* (New York: Doubleday, 2001), 45.

86 "Maybe down the road": Quincy Jones, interview with the author, October 1, 2018.

86 "My promise still stands": Quincy Jones, letter to Alice Walker, November 6, 1983, personal collection of Alice Walker.

5. READY TO WALTZ ON DOWN TO HOLLYWOOD

87 in her journal: Walker, *The Same River Twice*, 18.

88 "I'm scared to do it": Joseph McBride, *Steven Spielberg: A Biography* (Jackson: University Press of Mississippi, 2010), 367.

88 "I came away from it": Glenn Collins, "New Departures for Two Major Directors," *New York Times*, December 15, 1985, 2:1.

88 "The whole thing about separation": Myra Forsberg, "Spielberg at 40: The Man and the Child," *New York Times*, January 10, 1988, 2:21.

89 "I did not want that": Susan Dworkin, "The Strange and Wonderful Story of the Making of 'The Color Purple,'" *Ms.*, December 1985, reprinted in Walker, *The Same River Twice*, 175.

90 "there was a possibility": Alice Walker, "Turning *The Color Purple* into a Movie," *The Color Purple* (Two-Disc Special Edition), dir. Steven Spielberg, Warner Home Video, February 18, 2003.

90 "right next door": Susan Dworkin, "The Strange and Wonderful Story of the Making of 'The Color Purple,'" *Ms.*, December 1985, reprinted in Walker, *The Same River Twice*, 176.

91 "he was one": Susan Dworkin, "The Strange and Wonderful Story of the Making of 'The Color Purple,'" *Ms.*, December 1985, reprinted in Walker, *The Same River Twice*, 176.

91 "to be good": Walker, *The Same River Twice*, 18.

92 "NO PRESSURE": Steven Spielberg, letter to Alice Walker, February 23, 1984, personal collection of Alice Walker.

92 "Venetian Blind": Elena Featherston, "The Making of 'The Color Purple,'" *San Francisco Focus*, December 1985, 96.

93 "has to be in her DNA." *The View*, "Steven Spielberg Talks with Whoopi Goldberg About His Latest Work," ABC Studios, March 2, 2016, https://abcnews.go.com/Entertainment/video/steven-spielberg-talks-whoopi-goldberg-latest-work-37344715.

93 "Celie is so far away from me": Roger Ebert, "Whoopi Goldberg: 'The Color Purple,'" *Chicago Sun-Times*, December 15, 1985, https://www.rogerebert.com/interviews/whoopi-goldberg-the-color-purple.

94 "feel less alone": Alice Walker, "Journal Entries," March/April 1984, in *The Same River Twice*, 48–49.

94 "written the poem": Alice Walker, "Letter to Quincy Jones," March 1984, in *The Same River Twice*, 140.

95 "She is free of everything": Alice Walker, "Letter to Quincy Jones," 141.

95 "alternative title for his film": Alice Walker, "Watch for Me in the Sunset, Or The Color Purple," screenplay based on the novel *The Color Purple* (June 15, 1984), in *The Same River Twice*, 60–136.

96 "process of screenwriting": *The Color Purple* (Two-Disc Special Edition), dir. Steven Spielberg, Warner Home Video, February 18, 2003.

96 "I know it was painful": Lucy Fisher, letter to Alice Walker, July 5, 1984, personal collection of Alice Walker.

96 "not the one Stephen loved": White, *Alice Walker*, 405.

96 "made into a film": Susan Dworkin, "The Strange and Wonderful Story of the Making of 'The Color Purple,'" *Ms.*, December 1985, 174–82.

97 "just different": Dworkin, "The Strange and Wonderful Story of the Making of 'The Color Purple.'"

97 come to life: Quincy Jones, letter to Alice Walker, 1985, personal collection of Alice Walker.

97 "If I'm going to kiss a woman": Dworkin, "The Strange and Wonderful Story of the Making of 'The Color Purple.'"

98 "I've lived Celie's life": Quincy Jones in "The Cast and Crew Interviews," *The Color Purple* (Two-Disc Special Edition).

98 "sharing the same surname": Margaret Avery in "The Cast and Crew Interviews," *The Color Purple* (Two-Disc Special Edition).

99 "She had a very small part": *The Color Purple* (Two-Disc Special Edition).

99 "unself-conscious, and relaxed": Alice Walker, "The Color Purple: A Synopsis for Film," in *The Same River Twice*, 50–56.

99 "who thought Tina Turner more appropriate": Alice Walker, "Journal Entry—On Location in North Carolina, the 58th Day of Shooting," August 16, 1985, in *The Same River Twice*, 155–57.

100 pursue acting for the rest of her life: "*The Color Purple* Reunion," *The Oprah Winfrey Show*, Harpo Studios, Chicago, IL, November 15, 2010.

100 "An airplane flying overhead": Featherston, "The Making of 'The Color Purple,'" 94.

101 "It was as if I were back home": Featherston, "The Making of 'The Color Purple,'" s92–94, 96–98.

101 "more and more platitudes": Alice Walker, "Journal Entry," June 5, 1985, in *The Same River Twice*, 150–52.

102 "I might drown": Walker, *The Same River Twice*, 24.

103 "He wasn't": Walker, *The Same River Twice*, 35.

103 "too John Wayne–ish": Alice Walker, "Some notes on The Color Purple film for Quincy, Menno, and Steven from Alice," *The Same River Twice*, 142–43. April 26, 1985.

103 "'When I read my script'": Walker, *The Same River Twice*, 35.

104 "my inexplicable illness": Walker, *The Same River Twice*, 35.

105 "One must suspect": Coalition Against Black Exploitation, "Action Bulletin," April 1985, from Alice Walker's personal files, in White, *Alice Walker*, 414.

105 "one taboo": Philip M. Taylor, *Steven Spielberg* (London: Batsford, 1992), 114.

105 "scars the scene": Walker, *The Same River Twice*, 119–220.

106 "Shug's love for Celie is first expressed": Alice Walker, "'The Color Purple' Liner Notes," in *The Same River Twice*, 144–48.

106 "when I was ailing": *The Color Purple*, dir. Steven Spielberg, Warner Bros. Inc., 1985.

6. LET THE FILM ROLL

107 Together at *Femmes Noires*: Mickalene Thomas, *Mickalene Thomas: Femmes Noires*, Art Gallery of Ontario, Toronto, Canada, November 29, 2018–March 24, 2019.

108 "she related to some of those women in it": Mickalene Thomas, interview with the author, December 28, 2019.

108 Sandra's young marriage: *Happy Birthday to a Beautiful Woman: A Portrait of My Mother*, dir. Mickalene Thomas, 2012; 2014, HBO Documentary Films.

111 "their form and substance": Armond White, "The Color Purple," *City Sun* (January 15–21, 1986), as republished in Peter Rainer, *Love and Hisses: The National Society of Film Critics Sound Off on the Hottest Movie Controversies* (San Francisco: Mercury House, 1992), 378–83.

113 "It looks slick, sanitized, and apolitical to me": Alice Walker, "Journal Entry, San Francisco," December 6, 1985, in *The Same River Twice*, 161.

113 "the book is plain": Janet Maslin, "Film: 'The Color Purple,' from Steven Spielberg," *New York Times*, December 18, 1985, C:18.

113 "filmmaking by the numbers": David Sterritt, "Spielberg Scrubs and Softens 'The Color Purple,'" *Christian Science Monitor*, December 20, 1985.

113 "There are some great scenes": "Review of 'The Color Purple,'" *Variety*, December 31, 1984, https://variety.com/1984/film/reviews/the-color-purple-1200426436/.

114 "From the moment this movie": Julie Salamon, ". . . As Spielberg's Film Version Is Released," *Wall Street Journal*, December 19, 1985, 20, 25.

114 "It portrays blacks in an extremely negative light": Jack Mathews, "Some Blacks Critical of Spielberg's 'Purple,'" *Los Angeles Times*, December 20, 1985.

114 "the movie is very degrading": *Alice Walker: Beauty in Truth*, dir. Pratibha Parmar, 2013.

115 "We must destroy *The Color Purple*": Louis Farrakhan, "Farrakhan on *The Color Purple*" (Chicago: AVC, Record and Tapes, circa 1986).

116 "lick at society's rejects": E. R. Shipp, "Blacks in Heated Debate over 'The Color Purple,'" *New York Times*, January 27, 1986, A:13.

116 "about any color": Jack Mathews, "Some Blacks Critical of Spielberg's 'Purple,'" *Los Angeles Times*, December 20, 1985.

116 "everyday selves": Shirley Chisholm, letter to Diane Abrams, October 17, 1985, personal collection of Alice Walker.

117 "Let the film roll": Shipp, "Blacks in Heated Debate Over 'The Color Purple.'"

117 "Every community event in the city felt like it was about The Color Purple,": Danny Glover, interview with the author, August 31, 2018.

117 "I had seen Danny": Steven Spielberg in "The Cast and Crew Interviews," *The Color Purple* (Two-Disc Special Edition).

118 "with a quick smile": Trudy S. Moore, "Danny Glover: Villain in 'Color Purple' Is a Kind Family Man," *Jet*, March 17, 1986, 28–31.

118 "the level of a healer": Alice Walker, "Letter to Danny Glover," March 6, 1986, in *The Same River Twice*, 211.

119 "to have to change that": Roger Ebert, "That's The Way It Is: 'The Color Purple' and the Oscars," March 1986, republished in *Awake in the Dark: The Best of Roger Ebert: Forty Years of Reviews, Essays, and Interviews* (Chicago: University of Chicago Press, 2006), 337–40.

120 "our butts kicked for doing it": Matthew Modine, "Whoopee, It's Whoopi," *Interview*, June 1992.

120 "our struggles": Alice Walker, "In the Closet of the Soul," in *Living by the Word*, 78–92.

120 helped or harmed the black community: *Tony Brown's Journal*, PBS, April 6, 1986.

120 "the most racist depiction": *The Phil Donahue Show*, KGW, Portland, OR, April 25, 1986.

121 "She has said that lesbianism is wonderful": *Alice Walker: Beauty in Truth*.

121 "drive such a diverse group of people nuts": Evelyn White, email to the author, July 26, 2019.

122 "It just lifted me above": Walker, *The Same River Twice*, 23.

7. THE SINGLE MOST DEFINING EXPERIENCE I'VE EVER HAD

127 " 'to restore myself' ": "Oprah's Teahouse," *O, The Oprah Magazine*, Spring 2008.

128 "was an option?": Nicole Nichols, email to the author, October 6, 2010.

129 "my own studio": "Oprah's First Audition for Steven Spielberg," *Oprah's Next Chapter*, December 02, 2012.

129 "before the bookstore closed": Oprah Winfrey, interview with the author, October 10, 2018.

131 "Scared": Barbara Grizzuti Harrison, "The Importance of Being Oprah," *New York Times*, June 11, 1989, 6:28.

131 "'those men's acts'": Jackie Rogers, "Understanding Oprah," *Redbook: The Magazine for Young Adults*, September 1993, 132.

131 "somebody believes you": Laura Randolph, "Oprah Opens Up about Her Weight, Her Wedding and Why She Withheld the Book," *Ebony*, October 1993, 130.

133 "drafting the novel": "Key to the Characters in *The Color Purple*," Alice Walker Archive, Emory University, box 51, folder 1.

135 "doing that film": Richard Zoglin, "Lady with a Calling," *Time*, June 24, 2001.

136 "fight in my own house!": *The Color Purple*, dir. Steven Spielberg.

137 "that white women do": Claire Olsen, "Interview with Steven Spielberg and the Cast of the Color Purple," 1995, https://www.youtube.com/watch?v=WoEjMlNh5mU.

137 "more palpable than Walker": Dinitia Smith, "'Celie, You a Tree!' Review of *The Color Purple*," *Nation* 235, no. 6 (September 4, 1982): 181–82.

138 "let some light in": "Oprah Opens Up About Her Abusive Childhood," *The Oprah Winfrey Show*, September 8, 1986, http://www.oprah.com/own-oprahshow/oprah-opens-up-about-her-abusive-childhood-video.

141 "maybe you can see it": Salamishah Tillet, "Oprah Winfrey on 'The Immortal Life of Henrietta Lacks,'" *New York Times*, April 16, 2017, AR:22.

143 "She is incomprehensibly Powerful": Alice Walker, "Oprah" typescript, 2002, Alice Walker Archive, Emory University, box 84, folder 34.

8. I WAS STRUGGLING WITH FORGIVENESS
AT THAT POINT IN MY LIFE

146 "to take *The Color Purple* to Broadway": Scott Sanders, interview with the author, July 2, 2019.

149 once and for all: Walker, *The Same River Twice*, 35.

150 "Scott Sanders can": Alice Walker, "Getting Alice to Sign On," in *The Color Purple: A Memory Book of the Broadway Musical*, ed. Lise Funderburg, Alice Walker, and Brenda Russell (New York: Carroll & Graf, 2006), 16.

150 "I knew that even if we did something together": Alice Walker, "Atlanta," in *The Color Purple: A Memory Book of the Broadway Musical*, 26.

150 "very good journey": Alice Walker, "Getting Alice to Sign On," in *The Color Purple: A Memory Book of the Broadway Musical*, 16.

153 "see her at rock bottom": Gary Griffin, "Sofia," in *The Color Purple: A Memory Book of the Broadway Musical*, 97.

155 "ready to go": Marsha Norman, "Any Little Thing," in *The Color Purple: A Memory Book of the Broadway Musical*, 59 .

156 "alongside leather jackets": "'Color Purple' Drawing Diverse Crowds,"

Today, June 6, 2006, https://www.today.com/popculture/color-purple
-drawing-diverse-crowds-wbna13170487.

156 "fans sparks into a steady flame": Ben Brantley, "One Woman's Awakening, in Double Time," *New York Times*, December 2, 2005.

158 "I was a bit snobbish": Patrick Healy, "Stripping a Southern Musical to Its Core," *New York Times*, August 18, 2013, AR: 4.

160 "within its restraint": Ben Brantley, "'The Color Purple' on Broadway, Stripped to Its Essence," *New York Times*, December 11, 2015, C:1.

160 "seemed to die before your eyes": Jesse Green, "The Color Purple Is One of the Greatest Revivals Ever," *Vulture*, December 10, 2015, https://www.vulture.com/2015/12/theater-review-the-color-purple.html.

162 "he's done all these things": Edie Abrams-Macht, interview with the author, August 1, 2018.

EPILOGUE: NOW FEELING LIKE HOME

168 "her writing that made it so revelatory": Nylah Burton, "Alice Walker's Terrible Anti-Semitic Poem Felt Personal—to Her and to Me," *New York*, December 28, 2018. https://nymag.com/intelligencer/2018/12/alice-walkers-anti-semitic-poem-was-personal.html

INDEX